"This book conveys the essence of the Catholic Gospel with clarity, power, and practical insight. Too many people make too little of the truth that we actually become—and grow up—as members of Christ's Mystical Body. Our salvation is more than forgiveness, or even healing. Christ comes to share our human nature—and empower us to share his divine nature (2 Pet 1:4). Only God could do this. The good news is Christ does this. Highly recommended."

— Scott Hahn —
Father Michael Scanlan, T.O.R., Chair of Biblical Theology and the New Evangelization, Franciscan University of Steubenville

"For many years now, Fr. Meconi has been 'radiating Christ' in all he does, whether in his lectures at St. Louis University, in his growing number of books, or in his significant conversations with students and others, and sacramental ministry. In this new book he brings the fruit of his years of study and life together in a very accessible manner. He knows that the purpose of our life is nothing less than union with God and the purpose of his life has become helping the rest of us realize this. Thanks be to God!"

— Ralph Martin —
Director of Graduate Theology Programs in the New Evangelization, Sacred Heart Major Seminary

"'We are called to receive Christ so as to become him, and this alone will determine our eternal destinies.' With this one pithy sentence Fr. Meconi gets to the very core of our

Catholic faith. To be a Catholic is to participate in the life and love of the Holy Trinity. In this time of confusion, fear, and despair, Fr. Meconi's account of the ongoing Incarnation is inspiring, hopeful, and stylistically worthy of a Chesterton or James Schall, S.J. It would be a great blessing for the Church if this book were to be widely read as the antidote to so many of our pastoral problems."

— TRACEY ROWLAND —
University of Notre Dame (Australia)

"Fr. David Meconi's *Christ Alive in Me* is the fruit of countless hours of study, teaching, and prayerful meditation. In this masterful work, the reader is initiated into the language of deification in the Christian tradition. But because of Fr. Meconi's attractive prose, you move between Sacred Scripture, the *Catechism of the Catholic Church*, the Church Fathers, and the Oxford movement (and its later heirs) with total delight. Along the way, the reader is formed not only to understand what it means to speak about deification. You begin to desire it, hoping that you too can become God's and thus become gods. In reality, this book is not just a study of a specific doctrine or teaching. It is an introduction to the whole Christian life."

— TIMOTHY P. O'MALLEY —
Director of Online Education, McGrath Institute for
Church Life, University of Notre Dame

·⟡·

SERIES EDITOR: FR. DAVID VINCENT MECONI, S.J.

Fr. David Vincent Meconi, S.J., is a Jesuit priest and professor of theology at St. Louis University where he also serves as the Director of the Catholic Studies Centre. He is the editor of *Homiletic and Pastoral Review* and has published widely in the areas of Church history and Catholic culture. He holds the pontifical license in Patristics from the University of Innsbruck in Austria, and the D.Phil. in Ecclesiastical History from the University of Oxford.

ABOUT THE SERIES

The great Christian Tradition has always affirmed that the world in which we live is a reflection of its divine source, a place perhaps torn apart by sin but still charged with busy and bustling creatures disclosing the beautiful presence of God. The *Living Faith* series consists of eminent Catholic authors who seek to help Christians navigate their way in this world. How do we understand objective truth in a culture insistent on relativism? How does one evangelize in a world offended when invited to something higher? How do we understand sin and salvation when so many have no real interest in becoming saints? The *Living Faith* series will answer these and numerous other questions Christians have today as they set out not only to live holy lives themselves, but to bring others to the fullness of life in Christ Jesus.

CHRIST
ALIVE IN ME

Emmaus Road Publishing
1468 Parkview Circle
Steubenville, Ohio 43952

Library of Congress Control Number: 2021939208
978-1-64585-138-7 hardcover / 978-1-64585-139-4 paperback /
978-1-64585-140-0 ebook

Cover design and layout by Emily Demary
Cover image: *Christ in Limbo* (1442) by Fra Angelico

CHRIST
ALIVE IN ME

LIVING AS A MEMBER
OF THE MYSTICAL BODY

FR. DAVID VINCENT MECONI, S.J.

EMMAUS
ROAD
PUBLISHING

Steubenville, Ohio
www.emmausroad.org

Dedicated with gratitude to Mike and Rita Mooney,
humble coworkers in this Great Vineyard.

·❖·

·✦·

In these times, when the word "post-Christian" is employed to describe many European countries, and when the growing number of "nones"—those who prefer not to identify with any religious denomination—make for much hand-wringing in Christian churches, this slim, yet buff, volume of Fr. David Meconi arrives like a refreshing west wind. If the dry east wind of our age carries questions as "Why bother with a dull, insipid Christianity?" or "What does Catholicism offer to make a communal commitment worth my time and effort?," Fr. Meconi here answers with a Christian teaching meant both to send an electrifying current through the lukewarm believer and to seize the attention of those walking away (or merely sleepwalking): God lovingly plans for our participation in his divinity; in fact, he has sent his Son to *deify* us—now!

Many scholars, captivated in their early studies by a particular idea or figure, suffer a long, if happy, servitude to this one absorbing discovery. David Meconi's prodigious writing reveals that he has been held spellbound by a theology of divinization, from his early work on St. Augustine to this present book. And we should raise a hymn of gratitude that he has been so mastered by this doctrine, for it is one that the Church needs to be reminded of repeatedly. Although the doctrine of *theosis* has been preached since the first post-Resurrection communities— and Fr. Meconi puts this on full display in these pages—it nonetheless seems to disappear from the religious imagination with the regularity of the sun on a blustery March day. God stooping from his Divine Nature to snatch up fallen humanity for a real share in his own holiness and power: Is this not a bit too much? Does not our experience of other Christians, not to mention the knowledge of own capricious hearts and lives, give the lie to divinization?

Yet, it is as sure a truth as the Incarnation itself. Fr. Meconi echoes a long and rich tradition in asserting that the *raison-d'être* of each human soul is to be a willing vehicle of the God-man's divinity. The sending of the only-begotten Son into the world announced God's desire to draw humans into a sharing in the Divine Life. For the baptized to smile skeptically at this reality of divine love inches toward blasphemy. *God's ways are not our own.* Meconi has written a book not only to persuade the reader about the theology of divinization, but also to identify it as a path for spiritual perfection which answers the deepest desire of the human heart. Perhaps most importantly for our era, Meconi reveals that this vision makes Christianity come alive as the greatest of *adventures*—the superlative narrative of courage, romance, and fulfilment.

I think it fair to say that the "universal call to holiness," a radical announcement in the Second Vatican Council's *Constitution on the Church* (*Lumen Gentium*, ch. 5), now permeates Catholic consciousness and culture. As a professor of theology at an undergraduate Catholic college, my students seem no longer surprised by this teaching: they have imbibed it (perhaps with their mother's milk) and recognize that they should be struggling rigorously toward holiness in their lives—and especially in the future careers and vocations they choose. They understand the task to grow in virtue and to engage in pious activities and devotions, so much so that one begins to worry about a *risorgimento* of pelagianism. "*Becoming holy*," as Fr. Meconi suggests, sounds much more palatable than what deification proffers, "*becoming like God*." The path of the latter demands a radical openness and vulnerability, for, as Thomas Aquinas reminds us, *solus Deus deificat*—"only God can deify." In divinization, the work depends upon the initiative of the Son and the Spirit's chastening and purifying activity within us. Christ desires that we risk allowing ourselves to be upended and carried out by the surging wave of Divine Life to unknown territories. To be sure, this divine activity requires cooperation, a cooperation that surrenders those places in our lives which we cling to almost greedily as "our own" and that yields a misguided reluctance to embrace our *beloved* status before the Lord. Deification is no abstract Christian teaching: it is the Lord's love stretching forth to create a nuptial union between an individual human life and his own. At the end of Charlotte Brontë's magnificent novel *Jane Eyre*, Jane speaks of the marital intimacy with her beloved Mr. Rochester as a sharing in, and a sharing out of, a single life, a single heartbeat. The transforming union of Christ with the baptized soul exceeds even this intimacy between great lovers. Fr. Meconi's writing provides practical markers in the navigation of this journey of deification and homecoming, noting signs by which the believer can measure growth into a fuller participation in the Divine Life.

Part of the splendor of this work is the way this doctrine is presented from a number of different angles, as if the author were turning a jewel over in his hands to observe it fully. No doubt this is a wise rhetorical strategy to make *theosis* more attractive to the hesitant; but Fr. Meconi is also *doing theology*, clarifying a significant mystery of Christian life.

Front and center (rightly so) is the underappreciated Sacrament of Baptism. If Christian amnesia about the profound depths of this paschal rebirth were finally overturned, perhaps the glorifying light of divinization would blind less often. When the believer gives over her living flesh to God in the waters of Baptism, Jesus comes into her body to enliven it and make it fruitful with his own life. The new creature (*nova creatura*) now pulsates with the Divine Life that Christ willingly shares. Meconi also unveils this doctrine of *theosis* by exploring the theological categories of gift and participation, by discussing the ecclesial reality of the Mystical Body of Christ, by pointing to the goal of becoming "other Christs" in the service of others, and by letting Mary, the Church's paradigmatic Christian, lead the way. Illuminating voices from the tradition grace these pages: Peter and Paul; the mellifluous words of the fourth-century Fathers; the teaching of ecumenical councils and the *Catechism*; and the thought of figures like John Henry Newman, C. S. Lewis, and Hans Urs von Balthasar. Such a bedazzling doctrine demands this poetic catena of witnesses. This "gathering-up" yields a fruitful harvest indeed.

Fr. Meconi came to the undergraduate campus at which I teach in 2018, delivering lectures on the topic of divinization. His spoken words produced a vivifying current among our students—and not only among Theology and Catholic Studies majors. For several semesters, students were raising the topic in class and desiring to write senior theses that would include the doctrine of divinization. Imagine this intrigue and enthusiasm, this wonder and desire for an "ongoing incarnation" spreading quietly through our parishes and communities. Signs of the kingdom would be emerging, as from the mist of early morning fog.

Michon M. Matthiesen

University of Mary

Bismarck, ND

March 25, 2021, The Annunciation

CHAPTER 1

IT IS CHRIST WHO LIVES IN ME
(GAL 2:20)

Years ago, during my theology studies at the Jesuit College in the beautiful Alpine town of Innsbruck, Austria, I flew up to Scotland to visit one of my Jesuit brothers in Edinburgh. Since he was engaged in a meeting one of the days of my visit, I decided to use these free hours to take the train up to the coastal hamlet of Fife and then make my way out to the University of St. Andrews. Not yet ordained, I was walking through the city center in simple, everyday clothing, strolling amiably and enjoying this beautiful medieval town.

Around midday, I was approached by a street preacher similar to those who fervently frequent busy university cities like this, whether it be in Scotland or Madison, Wisconsin, Ann Arbor, Michigan, or Oxford or Paris. This very loving woman walked directly up to me and after a quick greeting, asked: "Do you have a personal relationship with Jesus Christ?"

"I do," I told her, "but I do not want one." Her mouth dropped. To be honest, my mouth kind of dropped as well. For I had never rehearsed such an answer before. It could have been her lovely Scottish accent, or it could have been the way she asked the question, but something in her reaching out to me certainly proved to be a true moment of grace.

What I heard myself saying was, "With you and with my friends, with the saints and with Mother Mary,"—by this point she had surely figured out that I was Catholic—"I would like to enjoy a relationship. But with Jesus Christ, I want something else. I do not want a relationship; I want something more. I want *union*. I want his words to become my words, the way he looks at people to become the way I look at people, for my heart to become his heart. I want his Incarnation to continue in me."

Without missing a beat, she instantly retorted in good Evangelical fashion, "That's not in Scripture."

"Sure it is," I assured her, paraphrasing Galatians 2:20: "I live no longer, but Christ lives in me." She looked at me astonished. This shabbily dressed American quotes St. Paul? We talked. We disagreed. We prayed together. As I turned away to get on with my sightseeing, it occurred to me that this impromptu answer, which surprisingly came from my mouth unrehearsed, was exactly what the Church Fathers called "divinization," "deification," or by its Greek term *theosis*.

This "en-godding," as the Anglican divine Edward Pusey (d. 1882) put it in a Lenten sermon late in his life, is not some esoteric document but an indispensable Christian tenet. In fact, as the following pages show, our giving God permission to dwell within us, thereby transforming us into another incarnate son or daughter, has been at the heart of the Christian Gospel for millennia. It is not just one theological doctrine among many, it is the ultimate and only goal of the entire Christian life. The only goal in God's becoming human is to continue his life in ours. In this new way of living our humanity, in Christ, the *Father is now able to love in us what he loves in his Son* because we too have been made to become Christ's other selves.[1]

So, why did I balk at this street preacher's invitation to a relationship with Christ? Well, we all know where our "lats" are—off to our sides. You see, the Latin word *latus* means "side" or "edge," and a re-*lation*-ship is, therefore, a side-to-side connection, an association based perhaps on a common history, similar tastes, and a desired future together as colleagues, friends, or maybe even husband and wife. It may be a connection forged between a moral agreement, it could be one based on shared desires and mutual plans, but the union Jesus Christ seeks for our souls is something much more personal and life-giving. In

---

[1] This italicized line is from the Catholic Mass, Preface VII for Sundays, and as we shall see below in ch. 6, such language runs all throughout the Church's prayers.

other words, Jesus Christ is not content staying on the *side* of our lives; he wants to be the vivifying as well as deifying source of all we wish to be and do. He is not content being just one relationship among many in our lives; he wants to be our life.

How does this conversion start? Do not worry. The initiative and agency in this process is wholly God's. These days we tend to use the word "seeker" for those who desire more wholeness and intimacy with the eternal. The more fundamental truth is, however, that we are not the seekers. We are the sought. It is God who is more committed to our perfection than we are; it is God who loves us and our children more than we do. It is he who desires our holiness and has done everything in his power to woo us into his own life. As such, any book of Christian theology or spirituality must begin with this awesome but often assailable truth: God is madly in love with you and desires your wholeness and your perfection. He is not disappointed in you, and he does not find you and your prayers a bother or distraction. That is the second foundational truth of the Christian faith: you are free, and the inestimable gift of free will, which God has given each of us, is intended for no other reason than that we come to Love and Truth willingly and joyfully.

Perhaps the third concept we need to mention, then, is the often-neglected fact that God has given us everything—from our mere existence to our favorite foods— for no other reason than that we use these immediate, concrete goods to foster a spirit of unbroken gratitude and see in the experiences of our lives the means by which we freely turn back to our loving Creator. This does not mean that you must become more "religious" or that you start to spend all day in Church, but that you first learn to see how, what the Psalmist calls the "desires of your heart" (Ps 20:5, 21:3, 37:4), your loves and passions, your family and career, your hobbies, and intimate companions along this way, have all along been the ways God intends to get your attention and win over your trust.

That is, all of these seemingly mundane gifts have been put into your life in order that you might savor God's goodness and, in response, lift every moment of your life up to him. In return he wants not simply to answer you, not simply to bless you, not simply to forgive you. He wants to transform you into someone superhuman, into someone saintly and wholly joyful. In short, he wants to make you into "another self," to continue to live his life in you, as you. He does this not by destroying your individuality and uniqueness but precisely by perfecting it in communion with the One who created you to exist in the first place.

This is possible because we are made in God's own image and likeness. Therefore, the more we become like

God, the more we become our truest selves. The Christian religion began not only in Jerusalem but with creation itself. That is to say, God made all persons—angelic and human—for intimate union, and the various manifestations of that original invitation, like creation or God's first covenant with the Jewish people, come to their fulfillment in the visible and all-consuming Incarnation of God into the human condition. When we see Christ, therefore, we see what it is that we have been created to become. Or as Vatican II teaches us, "The truth is that only in the mystery of the incarnate Word does the mystery of man take on light," and that is why Jesus Christ reveals not only the Father to us but also "reveals man to man himself and makes his supreme calling clear." (*Gaudium et Spes* §22).[2] This is something we can often put aside: the God-man reveals to us both who God is and who we too were intended to be.

So, for those who live in Christ, the glib phrase "to err is human" will seem somehow off. It is not human to err; error and decay, death and destruction are not what it means to be human, but they are less than what it means to be fully alive. For those who live in Christ are given the power to become people fully whole and free of self-doubt and loathing, children of God, friends to all, a Church so

---

[2] Second Vatican Council, Pastoral Constitution on the Church in the Modern World *Gaudium et Spes*, (December 7, 1965), §22.

inflamed with the truth and joy of the Father's love and the Holy Spirit's presence that we can now love our enemies, pray for our persecutors, so alight with the divine that we can pray in solitude amidst any storm, can walk on water, and even defeat death. This is what it means to be fully human, and this is who we are called to be.

The entire point of Christianity, then, is to have our souls melt before the fire of God's love. This call to divine intimacy means that we must surrender ourselves and all of the broken fissures in our souls to Jesus. For the Son of God has come to earth, comes to each of us, not only that he might heal us, not only that he might teach us, not only that he might save us, but he lives and longs to deify us. What he wants to do is to live our lives and, in return, have us live his life. He wants to become so one with each of us that his heavenly life finds a welcoming and familiar place within our souls and our souls consequently begin to manifest the life of Christ to all those we meet here on earth. This is the "great exchange," that in his humanity, the Lord offers us his own divinity.

An analogy will help. Think of a piece of iron. Alone, a piece of iron is hard and resistant. But if that piece of iron is put into a fire, it takes on a new nature, It does not cease being iron, but now it shares in the luminosity and the heat of that flame. In that fire, the iron now takes on dimensions: it becomes aglow, it becomes malleable and able to be worked into whatever the craftsperson needs. This is our soul in Christ. Alone and apart from our Creator, we remain hard and recalcitrant. But as we allow ourselves to let divinity enrapt us, we do not cease to be human, but we take on a new nature not our own: we become illumined and manageable in the Father's hands. We take on a new life that elevates and thus perfects our humanity as we now come to realize what the meaning of life and our existence has been all along.

That is what these ten chapters want to help us all understand more deeply: God became human so we humans could become god-ly. This two thousand-year-old Christian theology of "becoming God" is really another way of saying:

- My truest self is realized only when I am intimately connected to and sharing in God's own Divine Life.
- Because I am made in God's own image and likeness, the more I become like God, the more I become my truest self.
- The goal of my earthly life must therefore be to surrender to God's presence and allow myself to participate in him by relying on his way of living—his words and thoughts and actions—and thereby putting to death any tendencies or actions in me which block him.

- When this happens, the scriptural images of becoming God's adopted child, of becoming an eternal co-heir of heaven alongside Jesus, of becoming a living temple of God's Holy Spirit will all become real and meaningful.

- Here I finally understand the whole point of the Incarnation: since the Son of God has taken my human nature to himself, my humanity is now empowered to do things "in Christ" that no mere human could—for example, I can love my enemies, I never need to give in to my own fallen passions and desires, I can live with joy and purpose and everlasting bliss, and so on.

We shall treat each of these themes in the pages to follow, but let us also be clear what "becoming God" is clearly not for the Christian:

- It is never my attaining equality with God.
- It is never the annihilation or absorption of my individual humanity into God.
- It is never a life separate or apart from God's allowing me to share in his divinity.
- My "becoming Christ" is only analogous to how God literally became human in Jesus Christ: while his divinity was a complete personal unity with humanity, my humanity only

partakes of God who remains always and forever separate.

- It is never a life I can attain apart from the
  Church and her sacraments, apart from Christ
  and his Community.

In many diverse ways, this theology of deification captures
the Catholic Church's entire message: from her understanding of the Trinity to the Incarnation to the Church
and all the Church's teachings.

Simply taking a swath of sections from the *Catechism
of the Catholic Church*, this message comes through in a
magisterial manner: Christ took to himself so perfectly,
he did for us: "All Christ's riches 'are for every individual
and are everybody's property' (John Paul II, *Redemptoris
Hominis* §11). Christ did not live his life for himself, but
for us" (CCC §519).[3] In so humbling himself, he opens up
for us a life wholly united to God himself and thus gives
the perfect "example to imitate, through his prayer he
draws us to pray, and by his poverty he calls us to accept
freely the privation and persecutions that may come our
way (CCC §520). In this way, we learn next how:

---

[3] All citations from Sacred Scripture as well as from the *Catechism of
the Catholic Church* (hereafter, CCC) will simply be cited in the text.
In citing classic primary texts with an ancient history, I have chosen
simply to cite the source and not include the modern version or the
critical text edition in Greek or Latin.

Christ enables us to live in him all that he himself lived, and he lives it in us. "By his Incarnation, he, the Son of God, has in a certain way united himself with each man" (Vatican II's *Gaudium et Spes* §22). We are called only to become one with him, for he enables us as the members of his Body to share in what he lived for us in his flesh as our model: We must continue to accomplish in ourselves the stages of Jesus's life and his mysteries and often to beg him to perfect and realize them in us and in his whole Church. . . . For it is the plan of the Son of God to make us and the whole Church partake in his mysteries and to extend them to and continue them in us and in his whole Church. This is his plan for fulfilling his mysteries in us. (St. John Eudes, quoted in CCC §521)

These ten chapters were written with the aim of helping you wake up to this theology of Christian deification. It is also the theology of the Mystical Body of Christ, a key and central part of the Christian faith that used to be stressed much more before today. This is a radical part of the Good News: Christ is not some distant figure the faithful will meet only one day after death; his Incarnation is still ongoing as mortal creatures allow him to live in and through them. He is, of course, primarily alive and present in his Body's sacraments, but his presence does not stop at the edge of the sanctuary or the Church door. He is also present in those we meet each day, in the Mystical Body he is forming at every moment.

Following this Introduction, chapter 2 begins with the beginning, naturally enough, and Genesis 1:26–27's teaching that we have all been created in order to image and be like the Triune God. What does it mean to be a created image and likeness? How does this help us understand who we fundamentally are? By returning to the beginning and to the pristine purity of heart with which we were created, we shall see the original glory of what it means to be a person, to be embodied, and to be set over the rest of God's good earth.

Chapter 3 turns to the classic phrase in ancient Christianity to explain this divine transformation, "to share in the divine nature" (2 Pet 1:4) and the metaphysics of what it means to be divinized by participating in God's Triune Life. What exactly does this starkly strange phrase really mean—to become gods? What does deification really entail, and how are we best suited to understand it? Here the metaphysical category of participation, as opposed to possessing, is key.

In chapter 4 we take up the essential question of our existence and attempt to answer just who this Jesus Christ really is. Here we should be acutely aware that none of us is saved by theology or a doctrinal phrase, but by a man.

We are redeemed not by propositions but by a Person. It is the presence of this man Jesus Christ within each of us that brings us to the goal and the joy for which we have been created. It is not a matter of figuring things out or a matter only of morality, but something much deeper, much more mysterious; it is a matter of allowing Jesus Christ to take up life within each of our souls.

St. Augustine argues that when the risen Christ tells Mary Magdalene not to hold on to him, he is signaling the coming of another divine Person. This is the descent of the Holy Spirit, and in chapter 5, we turn to St. Paul's phrase at 1 Corinthians 6:19 and what it means to start living as God's holy temples. When God became human, he announced that his presence was no longer something geographical or spatial. He was no longer to be met only in the Temple of Jerusalem. He would now dwell in all humans, communicating his Divine Life, his gifts and fruits, through his Spirit of indwelling.

Only in this Spirit can we cry out, "Abba, Father" (Rom 8:15). Who calls another "Father" but his children? This filiality overflows, enabling us to call Mary our Mother and all the saints our brothers and sisters. In this Spirit we can begin to discern the truths of God and thereby become familiar with how God speaks to each of us as his own beloved and unique children. Chapter 6 opens with the greatest question any human can ever be asked: God's inquiring into who we say he is (Matt 16:15). In coming to know Christ so as to appropriate Christ in liturgy and in our own personal prayer, we finally come to understand the Church's theology of the Mystical Body. When we have a good sense of the theology of divinization, prayer and our reception of the sacraments change. We no longer simply ask for "things," but we begin to ask and to act for greater intimacy and surrender.

In chapter 7, we showcase C. S. Lewis's image of becoming "little Christs." Christ promises that whoever listens to his faithful ones listens to him (see Luke 10:16), and Lewis stands out today as one of the most faithful representatives when it comes to the basics of the Christian faith. Of all the themes found in Lewis, we shall concentrate on one of the most significant Christian works of the last one hundred years, Lewis's *Mere Christianity*. In so many rich and unmatchable ways, this work must be read as a complement to what we are expounding here, Lewis's insistence that the only real aim of Christianity is to become a "little Christ."

The divinized life must affect deeply how we choose to act, and in chapter 8 we use Matthew 25:40 to see how we are called to see and serve Christ in the least of his brothers and sisters. There is an ugly split between "social justice" and personal piety, and a theology of the Mystical Body offers the tools to mend that breach. We have a duty to serve the poor because we have the Gospel mandate to see Christ in the most forgotten. It is here, among the destitute and the great sinners, that our Lord felt most at home. We, too, must let our prayer and spiritual reading influence how we allow the beggar to approach us, how we spend our time and money, and how we live the years given to us on this crazy and oftentimes confusing earth.

Of course, none of this is possible without the Lady of Luke 1:28: Mary, full of grace. As we will have seen, by virtue of our incorporation into her Son Jesus Christ, Mary also becomes, in the words of Vatican II "our mother in the order of grace" (*Lumen Gentium* §61). In her "yes," God is allowed to enter his own good creation. Chapter 9, therefore, treats Mary's role in bringing the Divine Life into the created order. Here all the cosmos hung in balance, awaiting Our Lady's free offer of her very life. Here is where God would finally become one with and finally have direct contact with that which he created so long before. The Master here stoops lower than his servants, taking up the fragility and the uncertainties of humanity in the womb of a vulnerable virgin.

Finally, chapter 10 picks up on St. Paul's beautiful phrase at 2 Corinthians 3:18 to explore how we might move "from glory to glory" concluding our study by offering a look at our role in advancing the vision laid out here. Why have we lost this sense of deification and of the Mystical Body? How do we rediscover it, discuss it, preach on it, bring this heart of the Christian message to the world as modern-day evangelists? Vatican II's "universal call to holiness" (*Lumen Gentium* §39) demands that each of the baptized have some sort of evangelical arsenal—"Always be ready to give an explanation to anyone who asks you for a reason for your hope" (1 Pet 3:15)—ready to help others see the saving beauty of Jesus Christ. This means that each of us, regardless of our state or occupation in life, all have a deeper vocation: to surrender to the God who made us in order that we may allow him to send his Son into our hearts, minds, and deeds, and thus continue the Incarnation of his Son as he builds up disciples and extends his Son's own Mystical Body through every region and area of humanity.

CHAPTER 2

MADE TO IMAGE AND IMITATE THE TRIUNE GOD
(GEN 1:26–27)

When I was five years old, my father became very sick. When I was seven, he died. The words spoken to me that day have stayed with me ever since. My mom came downstairs where I was playing with my siblings in the basement, and she said, "Dad had a heart attack and won't be coming home." We knew he had been ill, but "Never coming home"? I was stunned, remembering how I simply stood there and looked at her. "How long is 'never'?"

"But now we have a job to do," my mother reassured us. "We can either be selfish and try to hold on to dad, or we can give him over to God the Father, and then we shall get them both back." While I obviously did not have the capacity then to understand what my saintly mother was really saying, I did see that she was not a total wreck. My mom was not crumbling, and I see why now. She never married my dad as her total completion, her ultimate fulfillment. She married my dad as an image of our eternal Father, an icon of Christ the Great Bridegroom, and so, when God decided to take my dad, albeit early, my mom did not fall apart. For it was never my dad's job to perfect my mom in the first place. Honestly, in some unbeknownst way, I think at that moment I found my vocation to the priesthood. Without every deprecating marriage and family life, I did come to see how no human marriage can ever truly and completely make us who we are created to be. If that is true, what, then, can satisfy us? What, then, is really the ultimate culmination of human existence?

Made for Divine Union

For centuries, Christians have started and stopped every public prayer by saying in common, "In the name of the Father, of the Son, and of the Holy Spirit." We begin prayer this way because these three names are the most immanent and eternal names for the three divine Persons of the Godhead. God's ultimate essence is love and, as St. Augustine recognized, wherever one sees love, one sees a trinity.[1] That is, wherever there is love, there must be a lover, the beloved, and the love who unites them. This is why "Father, Son, and Holy Spirit" are the most primal names for the Godhead because they bespeak the most inner-life of God as a perfect community of other-centered charity.

---

[1] Augustine, *On the Trinity*, 8.8.12.

Nowhere do we read "God is love" (1 John 4:8) in the Old Testament. Love is not one of the ninety-nine official names for Allah in Islam. This does not make Christians more loving, mind you, but it does expose an essentially different understanding of who God most intimately is. Only Christians can call God "love" because only Christians understand that God is not a force or a singular being, but a Trinity of Lover, Beloved, and the Love who eternally unites them. Love is never solipsistic; love is not monistic; love is never lonely. Love demands the presence of three—Father (Lover), Son (Beloved), and Holy Spirit (Love). There is no other reality like this: love is not an emotion or a feeling, but a communion of Persons so other-centered that the existence of each actually effects the identity of the others.

In time, God will eventually reveal himself to us as Creator, Savior, and Sanctifier, along with many other names, but his personal identity as Father, Son, and Holy Spirit is timeless and eternal because it best captures the fact that God is neither a monad nor in need of creation to be who he is. He was not eternally lonely before he created, nor was he void of intimate interpersonal communion. This is what God is, namely, a Love so other-centered, vulnerable, and transparent that the names Father, Son, and Holy Spirit most accurately reveal the ultimate nature of all of reality: that all things are brought about by love and that those made in this Trinity's image and likeness will become truly themselves only by imitating this triune movement of love.

When, for example, a human male sires a child, we can only then call him "father," but usually, he has had decades of existence and identity before that splendid moment. A human child is instantly son or daughter, but even that basic distinctiveness does not determine everything about this person, as he or she will grow to be brother or sister, friend, student, spouse, and so on. But the Persons of the Trinity are qualitatively different than what we experience as creatures. We have, built into our being, a unique autonomy that is not determined by any other human: we might be affected by others, but no one human person can *effect* us and determine our entire identity.

It is not that way in the Trinity. The First Person is who he is as Father only because he has a Son. If it were not for the Son, how could he be "Father," and if it weren't for the Second Person of the Trinity, how could there be a First? Also, the entire identity of this Second Person of the Trinity is filial only because he is begotten from the Father; the Son has no identity other than the fact that, as the Nicene Creed celebrates, he is "God from God, Light from Light, true God from true God." The same goes for the Holy Spirit: he is the Love between the Lover Father and the Beloved Son, without whom his identity as the bond of communion or the Gift between a Giver and a Receiver could not be at all. Where you and I might be partially dependent on others, and certainly are, this foray into Trinitarian theology shows us that the divine Persons are actually 100 percent dependent upon one another to be who they are.

The prolific Capuchin theologian, Fr. Thomas Weinandy, O.F.M. Cap., illustrates this paradox of divine "need" quite eloquently:

> For human beings not to be completely constituted by their relationships may first appear to be a good thing. Human persons possess an independent integrity apart from their relationships. However, it is precisely this independent integrity which does not allow a human person to be given completely to another, but he or she must do so only through mediating words . . . and actions. . . . The persons of the Trinity are eternally constituted in their own singular identity only in relation to one another; and they subsist as who they are only within their mutual relationships. In their relationships to one another each person of the Trinity subsistently defines, and is equally subsistently defined by, the other persons.[2]

---

[2] Thomas Weinandy, O.F.M. Cap., *Does God Suffer?* (Notre Dame, IN: University of Notre Dame Press, 2000), 117.

Back in the early fifth century, St. Augustine of Hippo wrote a lengthy work called *On the Trinity* (*De Trinitate*) and there coined a term "substantial relationship," which is precisely what Fr. Weinandy is inviting us to think about here.

St. Augustine is picking up on a distinction first made by the ancient Greek philosopher Aristotle (d. 322 BC), who showed how things could both change and stay the same. Over the years, I have grown taller (and wider!), but I am still the same person I have always been. I have changed, not substantially, but "accidentally," as Aristotle put it. The tree outside my office window has grown, and its leaves change annually, but it really is the same tree. In Aristotle's mind, then, a "substance" is precisely what a thing is, while those everyday changes and movements like age and size and place are what he calls "accidents," those non-essential qualities which inhere in a thing but do not totally define it.

Given this philosophical background, it is intriguing to think of the relationships between God the Father, the Son, and the Holy Spirit not as "accidental"—the way my friends and family have affected me but could never totally define me—but as "substantial." While I have had people come in and out of my life and I have remained basically the same, that is not how personal relationships are in the Trinity. The Father's entire personal identity, for example, is determined by the fact that he begets a Son. The Father has no other personality apart from his Begotten Beloved. As creatures, you and I have our own humanity: we are a lot alike, but your experiences and history and desires are not mine. Because each of us instantiates our own humanity, we have a solitude built into ourselves that we may, at first blush, think is a good thing.

Shamefully, we often use our individuality as a sort of existential asbestos, which does not allow others in fully. How often we can revel in our independence and aloofness in belonging entirely to another. But it is not that way in God. The Persons of the Trinity, while wholly and entirely distinct—the Father has his own intellect, will and consciousness, as do the Son and the Holy Spirit—share perfectly and fully one Divine Nature. Whereas you and I possess our own humanity, the divinity of the Triune God belongs to each divine Person equally. The only difference between the three is not *what* they are, for each is wholly God. The only difference between the three is *who* they are in relationship to one another. The relationships between them are what define each one personally: one is the Father/Begetter God, one is the Son/Begotten God, and another is the Holy Spirit/Given God. Accordingly, the personal identity of each Person is eternally actualized by the presence of the other two. For how could the Father be "Father" without a Son? How could one be "Son" without a Father, and how could there ever be a Gift without both a Giver and a Receiver?

This is the paradox: the Persons of the Trinity are more in "need" of one another than you and I are in need of those closest to us. But this only proves the paradox of love, a relationship that is so other-centered, it makes each person who he most fully is. To bring this home a bit, ask yourself: How many people in my life do I feel comfortable saying, "I love you" to? As high or as low as that number might be, it is certainly more than those to whom each of us can truly say, "You know? I not only love you, but I need you! I need you in order to be the best 'me' I can be." This is the paradox of true charity: it forges a shared identity between lover and beloved. Love compels one to see one's weal and woe in another. Your joy becomes mine; your tears become mine. This is not only the essence of the Trinity, it is also the entire point of the Incarnation: God loves us so much, he chooses to become like us. That is why he can instruct us that whatever we do to one another, we do to him. That is why Saul, persecuting the first generation of Jesus's followers, hears from the heavens, "Saul, Saul, why are you persecuting me?" (Acts 9:4). The Lord lets Saul know that he is not simply attacking his followers or his friends, but these faithful martyrs are actually continuations of Christ's own love on earth.

"The mystery of the Most Holy Trinity is the central

mystery of Christian faith and life. It is the mystery of God in himself. It is therefore the source of all the other mysteries of faith, the light that enlightens them" (CCC §234). Grasp the awesomeness of this teaching: the Trinity is not some abstract theological dogma, it is actually the pattern and the purpose of every aspect of our faith life. We are made in a Trinity's likeness, and the ramifications of this triune imprinting upon our souls are innumerable. One lesson the doctrine of our being created in God's own divine image and likeness teaches us is that this rebirth into our becoming God's adopted children was something he already prepared for at the world's beginning. Having been created in and for God, when we finally allow God to dwell freely in our souls, we become who he truly created us to be. It is the unfilled *imago Dei* (image of God) that is less than its intended state; we have all been created with that divine imprint, that godly capacity, in the center of our souls, a space which is, of course, not physical but existential in that our entire existence comes from and is heading back toward the One who alone Is (Exod 3:14). This is what it means to be a creature, to have our nature given to us, to be receivers of a giver, the bride to the groom, the patient to the agent. God is being, we are becoming. But in his infinite graciousness, God also created us with the ability to cooperate freely with him in the formation of our truest selves.

We have been granted the dignity of collaborating in our own character formation, our own identity and, yes, even our own destiny. We are made not only divinely-imaged, we are also created with the gift of free will, which means I can either choose to let Love form me or I can perpetually turn away. As Augustine put so beautifully, God, of course, had to create me without my permission, but he refuses to save me without my freely allowing him to: "But God made you without you. You didn't, after all, give any consent to God making you. How were you to consent, if you didn't yet exist? So while he made you without you, he doesn't justify you without you. So he made you without your knowing it, he justifies you with your willing consent."[3] Love never forces the other's assent; love never demands or makes ultimatums. Have you ever prayed, "Heavenly Father, Precious Jesus, Holy Spirit, I allow you to love me"? The Triune God's only desire in creating others like him was that they would freely turn toward him in joy and purity of heart, recognizing in him the beautiful reality of relationship, and thus long to become ever more like this Triune Love.

Since it is against God's goodness to force love, to drag free beings into his presence, we must cooperate with the grace he offers so as to grow in the ways he asks. For this, God began with the beauty of creation as his first

[3] Augustine, *Sermon* 169.13.

invitation to those made to know him. When we sinned, however, and began to destroy the integrity of the natural order (Gen 3), God began various covenants with the holy patriarchs of the Old Testament, and when those failed, God raised up his priests, sent the prophets, and gave Israel the monarchy they sought, but nothing was able to rouse the chosen people to proper holiness. All of these devices were God's acting from afar, but the Trinity finally decided to come to us as one of us: "In times past, God spoke in partial and various ways to our ancestors through the prophets; in these last days, he spoke to us through a son, whom he made heir of all things and through whom he created the universe" (Heb 1:1–2). The Father sent his Son to enter his creation in a way he had never done before, as a creature. In uniting this created condition to himself, God has changed—not himself—but all of creation. This is the beginning of salvation, as the initiative is always Love's prerogative. It is in this dynamic of Love we are made, so let us now examine more in depth three aspects of this gift.

Image as Fulfillment: Made for Triune Love

The first thing to consider when reading that we are made in God's image and likeness is to see that we are the only creatures created so. When looking at this part of the story in Genesis, the council fathers gathered at Vatican II came to teach that the human person, "the only creature on earth which God willed for itself, cannot fully find himself except through a sincere gift of himself" (*Gaudium et Spes* §24). According to one of the highest teaching offices of the Catholic Church, then, you and I are the only creatures God created simply for the sake of our own existence. After all, which one of us would rejoice knowing we were created for the sake of something else?

That is the fate of lower creatures: God created the earth for dirt, dirt for grass, grass for cows, and cows for us, and so on. We humans simply *are*; we have no other reason to be—the way a mother passes hours upon hours simply gazing upon the face of her newborn child. That baby absorbs all her attention, saps all her energies, and she delights in nothing other than this little one who does nothing other than rest in her arms. That is the first truth of Vatican II's teaching: human persons exist for no other reason than God willed us to be.

That being the case, then, the second truth contained in this clause teaches that we are the only creatures who fulfill their nature by learning to become sincere gifts. This may at first shock us, but our lives are not given to us fully-formed. This means human living can go wrong. No other creature has such a drama built into its life. But while those sub-human creatures may never err in being a tree or in being a salmon or a stork, they will also excel only so much. Yet we who are endowed with free will can realize eternal perfection. We may have the risk of damnation, but God offers us his very self. This is why we must learn to let our human nature imitate God's own self-giving. The only other option is allowing our natures to implode and thereby neglect God's invitation by becoming self-centered, self-loathing failures. Unlike other created lives, human living is an all-or-nothing event: it either attains the celestial glories of heaven or falls into the nameless depths of despair. There is no other possibility.

This is why it is essential to realize what it means to be made in the image and likeness of the Almighty. If the Triune Life is the final goal of our existence, attaining that goal freely and faithfully demands our cooperation in learning what the goal and guide of human flourishing is: first, to realize we are made to become gift for the other and, second, to learn precisely who this other is. This is how Christian holiness is not something God thought of only after we had turned away from him. Our innate invitation to godliness was not a result of the Fall but was built into the way God created Adam and Eve and every human person since. The sinfulness of humanity may have changed the way by which we become holy—now only through the cross of the Crucified Christ—but God's desire and our thirst for divine union were already present in the first moment of human existence. For in creating us in his image, God "stamped" us with an imprint of himself from the very beginning.

This is why this world leaves us wanting. It is not that creatures—ballgames, human friends and acquaintances, meals, and vacations—are ever bad. Given our eternal lifespan, they're just incomplete. The thirst derives not from the meagerness of created goods, which would only foster a sense of snobbery and arrogance on our part. At the end of the day, we realize that we are made for much more than the good things which surround us, because we have been made to be eternally in union with Perfection himself:

> What else does this craving, and this helplessness, proclaim but that there was once in man a true happiness, of which all that now remains is the empty print and trace? This he tries in vain to fill with everything around him, seeking in things that are not there the help he cannot find in those that are, though none can help, since this infinite abyss can be filled only with an infinite and immutable object; in other words by God himself.[4]

We are conceived with a divine hunger, with a "God-sized hole" in our hearts that only God can fill, or as St. Augustine's famous opening to his *Confessions* put it, "Our

---

4   Blaise Pascal, *Pensées*, trans. A.J. Krailsheimer (New York: Penguin Books, 1966), 75, section VII, 425, under "Morality and Doctrine."

hearts are restless until they reset in you, O God."[5]

Unfortunately, many of us spend way too much of our lives trying to figure out what exactly the point of human existence is—in other words, in whose image and likeness are we made. When we get the answer to this question wrong, our psyches split, and we spend our lives trying to figure out what brings us ultimate meaning and thus worth. Like St. Augustine, we can spend years and years trying to find that place of rest the world's most famous convert longed for so deeply and so much more eloquently than most of us. Yet, like this fourth century rascal, our search is the same. For if we think we are made in the image and likeness of civic and public honor, we are always going to feel slighted; if we think we are made in the image and likeness of sexual pleasure, we are always going to feel unloved; if we think we are made in the image and likeness of financial success, we shall never feel we ever have enough.

Image as Invitation to Holiness

But as sons and daughters of our first parents whose first home was the Garden of Eden, we carry about us a faint trace of that same desire to live in a world without strife and division. We, too, long for perfection, but despite what modern ideologies tell us—and what the saints have

---

[5] Augustine, *Confessions*, 1.1.1.

proven to us—the unalloyed joy we all desire will be found only in Christian holiness. This comes not from denominational arrogance or Christian superiority. We are all made for goodness, and only union with the Good can calm and consummate our lives.

Have you ever noticed how the correct choice, at some moment of real virtue, just "feels" good and satisfying, resulting in a certain enthusiasm, transparency, and possibly a desire to share with others what just occurred? On the other hand, an unfortunate moment of vice usually brings shame and a certain sorrow, regardless how alluring that word or action may have seemed at first, locking us in on ourselves, hopeful that no one else finds out something we surely will not be broadcasting. This is because you and I are made in "the image and likeness" of Goodness, of Truth, of Beauty. One need not be a Christian to catch a glimpse of this reality.

But we currently live in an age where we fight against the indisputable reality that a particular nature has been given to us. None of us has caused ourselves; our existence is total gift. Our human nature, our bodies, our gender, our world are all gifts which we manipulate only at our own peril. As gift, these have been given, and our humanity (and all it entails) has been given to us by One who desires we fulfill that nature properly, but who has also given us the gift of free will by which we can either receive or reject what it means to be human—what it means to be rational, what it means to be male or female, and so on. We Americans especially want to determine not only everything we do but everything we become. We have so sadly voted in laws that aim to do this and persons who are intent on usurping the Creator's role and determine the worthiness of the unborn, the dignity of weakened and aged life. Not surprising, from this tyranny come laws which now determine the nature of marriage and even now statues that determine the God-given gender of my body and how others must respond to my choice. We live in an age where the individual will is sovereign. But the ancient stories of human civilization have offered another account of how things should be.

As creatures we all need to accept that our existence, our nature, our purpose—not to mention our minds and bodies, individual capacities, much of our identities— have all been given to us. None of us caused ourselves, no creature can grant itself existence, no creature can determine its God-given nature. These are humbling truths the proud simply cannot admit. So, if all is gift, it is not we who determine reality, but we are instead invited to receive what is real. This is the beginning of holiness, what the Scriptures and the saints call spiritual poverty. "Blessed are the poor in spirit, for theirs is the kingdom of heaven" (Matt 5:3). This is the type of poverty that saves us, allowing us to go through life realizing deeply that everything has been donated to me so I may fulfill some particular purpose, offer God some particular life that no one on else could ever live. This is why each of our lives matter ultimately and eternally. Only I could have lived this life God gave me; only I could have had influence on these people, at this address, and during these decades. My life, my family, my circle of friends, and so on—only I could have been that husband or wife, father or mother, confidant or colleague to them, and that is why the Lord created me when and as he did. To be mindful of this is to increase our awareness of the incessant providence of God, while also coming to recognize very concretely and particularly the purpose of my unique existence.

At every Mass, Christians are instructed to, "Lift up your hearts," to which we respond, "We lift them up to the Lord." This is no mere phrase but an instruction to live as we were meant to be, as terrestrial beings whose identities are at the same time heavenly. For this we on earth have been made: we have become so accustomed to the pressures and demands of this world that we often forget that God's divine gifts have been given to us so we could live in this busy world with heaven always in mind. We are made for holiness, and this notion inspires every teaching of Christianity. "What profit is there for one to gain the whole world and forfeit his life?" (Mark

8:36). The holiness that comes from Christ is the only gift which can satisfy our deepest longings. And among the most beautiful things about this teaching in a healthy Christian context is that holiness does not mean leaving the world but allowing oneself to be in the world not only for or with Jesus but actually as Jesus.

When we are young, we might think of doing things for Jesus or Mary, for a Jesus and a Mary who are "out" there in the heavens. We might perform small acts of virtue or offer up some deed or dislike for the Lord and all the saints who gaze down upon us from heaven. When I was a young boy, I would sometimes walk to St. Mary's grade school after having placed a pebble in my shoe and all the time imagine Jesus looking down on me and being so happy with the small shots of pain in my foot. I would look up and let Jesus know at every step that I was doing this *for* him. When we get a bit older, we might imagine Jesus and Mary being alongside us, *with* us, offering their grace and leading us through all the stresses of adult life. The image here is being buttressed by divine support by those who have walked this life as well.

But there is a higher proposition, a higher preposition: to do these things *as* Jesus or Mary would. Imagine what our life would be like if we met those we meet every day *as* Jesus or Mary would meet them; if we treated our spouse and children *as* Jesus or Mary would; if we approached the Father in the perfect confidence of his love *as* Jesus and Mary do. Allowing God and his saints to enter our souls and thereby transform us into another generation of living icons of Christ is what we have all been created for and what alone can make sense of every aspect of the human condition.

Image as Steward and Dominion

As the apex of God's visible creation, we human persons have been charged with working out our salvation as ones who have been charged with care over God's creation. We are his living stewards who are to tend and take care of what he has freely given us.

> God created mankind in his image; in the image of God he created them; male and female he created them.
>
> God blessed them and God said to them: Be fertile and multiply; fill the earth and subdue it. Have dominion over the fish of the sea, the birds of the air, and all the living things that crawl on the earth. God also said: See, I give you every seed-bearing plant on all the earth and every tree that has seed-bearing fruit on it to be your food; and to all the wild animals, all the birds of the air, and all the living creatures that crawl on the earth, I give all the green plants for food. And so it happened. (Gen 1:27–30)

Being immersed in this world of "male and female," of fish and birds and living and crawling things, we sometimes forget that this is the way God originally devised our wholeness, through the very mundane experience of being embodied, eternal beings.

The Catholic Church has always seen the material as the place where the divine is met. The goodness of this wildly wonderful creation was God's first gift to us, but he never intended to leave us at a distance. A characteristic of love is the desire to draw close to one's beloved, and in his Incarnation, God assumes human flesh and blood personally and eternally to himself. In his Church, God continues to embed himself in the divine vehicles of water, oil, bread, and wine, and all the other sacramentals— rosary beads, Miraculous Medals, scapulars—which speak to us of God's closeness.

But for the first time, the Church's official teaching is finally sensing the Spirit's inspiration to address the fragility of all these gifts and our call to take care of the creation the Father has assigned to us children. In his not unquestioned 2015 encyclical *Laudato Si'*, Pope Francis turned the Church's attention to what many perceive as an ecological crisis today and how we Christians really should lead the charge to foster a loving dominion and care over the earth with which God has entrusted us. In a work many found controversial, Pope Francis never borders on pantheism nor does he equate the subhuman beasts with the glorious children of God.

The title of this ground breaking encyclical, "May He Be Praised" in English, comes from St. Francis of Assisi (d. 1226), our saintly paragon of one for whom God's creation mattered so much. Throughout Pope Francis's writing, in fact, one can hear the wit of G. K. Chesterton who reminded us a century ago that,

> The main point of Christianity was this: that Nature is not our mother: Nature is our sister. We can be proud of her beauty, since we have the same father; but she has no authority over us; we have to admire, but not to imitate. This gives to the typically Christian pleasure in this earth a strange touch of lightness that is almost frivolity. Nature was a solemn mother to the worshipers of Isis and Cybele. Nature was a solemn mother to Wordsworth or to Emerson. But Nature is not solemn to Francis of Assisi or to George Herbert. To St. Francis, Nature is a sister, and even a younger sister: a little, dancing sister, to be laughed at as well as loved.[6]

Creation and we have the same Father, although he imprinted his own image and likeness into those he would

---

[6] G. K. Chesterton, *Orthodoxy* (New York: Dodd, Mead and Company [1908] 1959), 207, under ch. VII, "The Eternal Revolution."

come to redeem in his Son, as his sons and daughters.

But he created us in this world of flora and fleece, of fish and fawns, this world of so many hues of greens and blues, of mountains and majestic sunsets, and it took the courage of Pope Francis to orient the Church's thinking on the topic of ecological awareness. Being made in God's image and likeness means that it is to us men and women that he entrusts the lower part of his creation, and this must somehow impact each of our spiritual lives. Or in the words of Pope Francis:

> A spirituality which forgets God as all-powerful and Creator is not acceptable. That is how we end up worshipping earthly powers, or ourselves usurping the place of God, even to the point of claiming an unlimited right to trample his creation underfoot. The best way to restore men and women to their rightful place, putting an end to their claim to absolute dominion over the earth, is to speak once more of the figure of a Father who creates and who alone owns the world. Otherwise, human beings will always try to impose their own laws and interests on reality.[7]

---

[7] Pope Francis, Encyclical Letter on Care for Our Common Home *Laudato Si'* (May 24, 2015), §75. For more on this in our series, see Christopher J. Thompson, *The Joyful Mystery: Field Notes Toward a Green Thomism* (Steubenville, OH: Emmaus Road Publishing, 2017).

Because God has placed us over his creation, he has entrusted the goodness of fragile existence to us, his images and likenesses in the visible order of reality. In so doing, the Father longs for us to meet him in and through his creatures but never to make them a substitute for him. Only in tending to their care are both goals met: we represent God on earth when we continue his role as Creator in tending to what he gives us, and we place all things rightfully under us when we participate in our call to dominion, always remembering that to have dominion is entirely different than to be charged with domination.

Like any loving parent, God is depicted in Genesis preparing our home (for five days!) until we are brought home. This great earthen nursery of God's primordial gift to us was carefully created and tended for all enjoyments and pleasures he willed to give us through the smells and sounds, the fauna and flora, the beasts and the beauty of Eden. Only then, only after all this was prepared just right, perfectly in fact—for that is what Eden represents—did he bring his children into the world.

That is why for Catholics especially, this world is a sacramental, lifting our eyes and hearts up to its Creator. The world is drenched with grace, with living reminders of God's lavish love, filled with existence itself, which only he, whose nature it is to exist, can grant. Only once we realize how this visible order of existence is God's first gift to his children can we be free enough to enjoy the goodness of creation instead of always being bogged down by the anxieties and cares of this world—stresses which are no doubt real, but which can become purposeful and salvific when offered to the Father in love and trust.

This why we are unique among all of God's creatures: angelic in our eternal and rational souls, animals in the movements and sensation of our bodies. We are thus images who microcosmically encapsulate all of God's good creation: heavenly in our souls and earthly in our bodies, intended to encounter the divine in the world of matter. St. Ambrose accordingly wrote that:

> Thus the soul that is unto the image of God acts not just by corporeal means, but by an acuity of heart that sees what is absent, in its gaze traveling across the sea, in its vision racing all over, investigating what is hidden, applying its senses here and there in a single instant to the ends of the whole earth and the secrets of the world; this is the soul that is joined to God, adheres to Christ, descends to Hell, and, set free, dwells in heaven.[8]

United to Christ, one with Christ, the Christian soul thus combines human nature—body and soul—with life in the Holy Spirit, thus adhering to Christ and thereby allowing

---

[8]   St. Ambrose, *Hexameron*, 6.8.45.

him to continue his Incarnation in each of the baptized. In him we, too, die, descend into hell, and are resurrected in Easter joy. This is what it means to be divinized, what it means to live the Christ-life.

Let us now continue this theme and examine more deeply what this type of deifying union really means. Where is it found in Scripture, and what does the Church actually intend by continually teaching, century after century, that in God's humanity is our divinity?

CHAPTER 3

SHARING IN THE DIVINE LIFE (2 PET 1:4)

The term "deification" is one that is not used very much. It can sound something of New Age spirituality. It can be very misleading. Perhaps it's too powerful. It is a combination of two Latin words *facere*, "to make," and *Deus*, "God." So, literally, it means "to be *made god*," but I often translate it as being *made god-ly*, and the fact that I have to add on that suffix shows the shock of such a theologically orthodox position. Become god? Me? But this, as all the great Church Fathers taught, is our only ultimate call in life. We today might tend to relax that call by qualifying what we mean—softening "becoming god," by saying "becoming godly," or "becoming holy," or other similar terms. There is nothing wrong in that, but it does avoid the impact the phrase "becoming god" was intended to have by the best of Catholic thinkers. Throughout the centuries of Christianity, the terms "deification" or "divinization"—or the Greek equivalent, *theosis*—are used consistently, and the reality of this teaching is clearly found throughout Sacred Scripture.

This chapter will lay out what is meant by these terms, where the reality is found in Scripture and where expressed in the *Catechism of the Catholic Church*, what divinization certainly is not, and why it really is the goal of the Christian life. Admittedly, the terms "deification" and "divinization" are not readily used in Christian circles these days. My sense is that most Christian sermons and homilies do, in fact, invoke the central, core beliefs of deification but instead use terms like "sanctification," "growing in holiness," "becoming children of God," or other equivalent concepts. Perhaps "deification," or "becoming gods," or even "becoming godly" smacks too much of a New Age pagan spirituality; perhaps it is too close to the Mormon doctrine of exaltation in which one literally becomes a deity. So, what does the ancient Christian Church mean by these terms? What, in fact, do faithful followers of Jesus mean by becoming gods?

What is meant by these provocative phrases is nothing other than the ultimate good news, namely, that God does not simply wish to create other persons, nor is he content simply saving us from sin. He created us in order to confer upon us his own perfection, his very own life, consisting of eternal joy and total self-gift where there can be no fear, no hurt, no loss. God has never been satisfied with simply leading us from afar. He has never been that impressed with our knowledge, however sublime, or with our virtue, however pristine. He wants to give us his own Divine Nature, to transform us into perfect lovers, a betterment that cannot be achieved by pure nature. This is clearly a divine act, and what it entails and what it does not entail is of the utmost importance.

What Is Meant by Deification?

This is a bold claim, but all the great Catholic thinkers, each in his or her own way, has taught a theology of deification. Throughout the ages the way this was achieved or how it was described may have varied, but any saint understands how Christ came to graft us onto his own life-giving self. St. Paul highlighted how this was achieved through our being adopted into the Father's family, the Church Fathers were a bit bolder and exhorted Christians to becoming god, the Medieval Doctors and Rhineland Mystics would talk about a certain fusion without confusion, or a union without an absorption. What the doctrine of deification wants to advance is an image of Christian salvation which sees how the mortal soul is being transformed to be one with God and thus partake of the Divine Life in a superhuman manner.

All of this is to say that our participation in the Divine Life is the solid and steadfast aim of all faithful Christian theologies. The terms and the methods suggested may vary, but the entire Tradition insists that to be saved is to dwell mutually in Christ in such a way that the creature is transformed into a member of his Mystical Body and therefore exhibits superhuman actions. As Christ continues and thus extends his Incarnation in each of his faithful who allow him to live their lives, these saints-in-the-making become more and more who they were originally created to be. This is the "great exchange," the Son of God's humanity for our share in divinity. This is the work of salvation, not following rules but a rebirth from which all the virtues and good works flow.

The first Christian to define *theosis* was a shadowy rogue who called himself Dionysius and tried to pass himself as the convert St. Paul made on the Areopagus Hill in Acts 17. Dionysius the Areopagite, or, more honestly, Pseudo-Dionysius, taught that deification was a participation in God's own Trinitarian life and thereby enabling us to "attain the likeness of God and union with him insofar as possible."[1] Participation is vastly different than possession. We cannot be godly without God, but this is precisely what Satan used as his diabolical gambit against the human race. The primal temptation was to seek eternity without the Eternal, to become perfect without Perfection himself. "You will be like gods" (Gen 3:5). But when we allow ourselves to live with God as

---

[1] Dionysius the Areopagite, *Ecclesiastical Hierarchy*, 1.3.

our very life, the union and subsequent likeness which emerges is a new life for us otherwise mortal sinners. In consciously and freely uniting our humanity to divine humanity, Christ allows us to live his life as he lives ours. As in the best of marriages or perhaps throughout the fragile pregnancy of any loving mother, we no longer think just about ourselves but begin to have another always in mind. We know our actions and decisions are not just ours, but they involve another whom we cherish, adore, and want to see safe and joy-filled. This is what Christ offers us if only we are willing to offer it back to him in return.

> It is plain that such an inhabitation brings the Christian into a state altogether new and marvelous, far above the possession of mere gifts, exalts him inconceivably in the scale of beings, and gives him a place and an office which he had not before. In St. Peter's forcible language, he becomes "sharer of the Divine Nature" (2 Pet 1:4), and has "power" or authority, as St. John says, "to become the son of God" (John 1:12). Or, to use the words of St. Paul, "he is a new creation; old things are passed away, behold all things are become new" (2 Cor 5:17). His rank is new, his parentage and service new. He is "of God" (1 John 4:4), and "is not his own" (1 Cor 6:19), "a vessel unto honour, sanctified and meet for the Master's use, and pre-

pared unto every good work" (2 Tim 2:21). This wonderful change from darkness to light, through the entrance of the Spirit into the soul, is called Regeneration, or the New Birth; a blessing, which before Christ's coming, not even the Prophets and righteous men possessed, but which is now conveyed to all men freely through the Sacrament of Baptism.[2]

Here one of the Church's most recently canonized saints, John Henry Newman (d. 1890) brings together all the major elements of divinization: It is entirely God's initiative and agency, it is a participating (not a possessing) in God's own life, and it renders one as an adopted son or daughter now endowed with a new identity and capacity for true righteousness, all granted through the Holy Spirit in the Church's gift of Baptism.

We have unfortunately lost today the beauty of this teaching. Christianity is a two-act play. The story begins with God becoming flesh. The shocking introduction is an awesome descent of the divine into his own good creation. But that is only the first half of a two-act play. In the second act, the creatures which the Son of God took to himself are now to become divine. In his emptiness is our fullness; in his humanity is our "divinity." This lan-

---

[2] John Henry Cardinal Newman, "The Indwelling Spirit," in *Parochial and Plain Sermons*, 2.19 (San Francisco: Ignatius Press, 1987), 366.

guage of exchange is not of the New Age or some kind of non-Christian fancy. When Christians rightly speak of "becoming God," what is meant is a sharing of natures and an admittance of a two-fold need. Since God could not die without becoming mortal, without taking into himself a created nature, he had to become a man in order to redeem us in the way he desired. Conversely, since we cannot truly live without placing ourselves in God's own life, we have to open ourselves up to a nature not our own, the Divine Nature, where we alone find what it means to be truly human. God could not die without us; we cannot live without God.

Sacred Scripture and the Catechism of the Catholic Church

It is not untrue that God's chosen people were the first monotheistic worshippers in the history of religions, the first recorded people who held out only one true God with no ultimate rival: "Hear, O Israel! The Lord is our God, the Lord alone" (Deut 6:4). Yet what is even more accurate is that these monotheists held that while the cosmos is full of competing deities, there is only one God worthy of right worship. For this reason, monolatrianism—the belief in many gods but the worship of only one God—is a more accurate description of what the early Israelites thought. In fact, one of their central Hebrew names for the Almighty, Elohim, means "the God of gods." This might help explain why a faithful Jewish person would celebrate the first time God calls a mere creature a god—for it meant that the one true Lord was going to share his power with one clearly below him.

When Moses argues with God that he is simply too ineloquent to persuade Pharaoh to release the Hebrews, God gets upset with Moses, assures him of Aaron's help, but then reminds him that the one true God has the ability to give others a share in his power and thus his name: Aaron "will speak to the people for you: he will be your spokesman, and you will be as God to [Pharaoh]" (Exod 4:16). And then a few chapters later, this promise is reiterated: "The Lord answered Moses: See! I have made you a god to Pharaoh, and Aaron your brother will be your prophet" (Exod 7:1). It is from this type of invitation into his own life that God gives his chosen people access to his own ability to rule over other worldly powers, to bless his people (see Exod 39:43), and to become "perfect" (see also Deut 18:13, DRA).

The most relied upon passage from the Old Testament comes in the center of Psalm 82 where the psalmist sings, "I declare: 'Gods though you be, offspring of the Most High all of you'" (v. 6), but then instantly instructs us that this is a godliness which is not inborn and intrinsic to the mortal but remains ever and always a gift that can be withdrawn at any time: "Yet like any mortal you shall die; like any prince you shall fall" (v. 7). As we shall see, this fits the pattern of orthodox teaching on Christian divinization. The saints—even Our Lady—are all mortal and in need of salvation (hers, of course, received at the moment of her conception) but will also be made children of the Most High, transforming them into sons and daughters of their heavenly Father.

As numerous as these allusions to deification are in the Old Testament, it is not until the revelation of Jesus Christ and our Father's plan to bring souls into his own Divine Nature that we finally receive fuller understanding into what this sense of salvation really means. Perhaps the most often cited passage comes from the Apostle, the pope, St. Peter, who was writing to his flocks across the Mediterranean. St. Peter teaches that with the graces of our new life in Jesus we partake of the Divine Nature, but we never possess it:

> His divine power has bestowed on us everything that makes for life and devotion, through the knowledge of him who called us by his own glory and power. Through these, he has bestowed on us the precious and very great promises, so that through them you may come *to share in the divine nature*, after escaping from the corruption that is in the world because of evil desire. (2 Pet 1:3–4, emphasis added)

This is the *locus classicus* of deification, *sharing in the Divine Nature*, providing the theological justification for a message that runs throughout the rest of the New Testament.

That message of Jesus's invitation for us to be like him can be found in various images, but the most prevalent are: (1) the great exchange language of God's humanity for our divinity, (2) the divine adoption metaphor stressing our co-heredity along with Jesus Christ, (3) becoming divinely conformed and thus elevated to do things that are superhuman.

The Great Exchange

The first image to examine fills out what St. Peter's passage just assumed: that we can share in God's nature only because he first shares in ours. All is gift, and we can give to God only what he has first given us. Therefore, we are able to participate personally in the Divine Life only because the divine had taken on our human life prior. St. Paul establishes this language of what has come to be known as the great exchange by teaching us that, "For you know the gracious act of our Lord Jesus Christ, that for your sake he became poor although he was rich, so that by his poverty you might become rich" (2 Cor 8:9). In emptying himself, the Son of God is able to lavish his life in the Father upon us. In so doing, he is not simply pouring grace extrinsically upon us, but he is transforming us from within.

In this emptying, what St. Paul here calls the Son's *kenosis*, there is a play on words in Greek which captures this great exchange: that our *theosis* is the Son's *kenosis*—in his emptying is our divine fulfillment. This is a fulfillment which the world cannot understand, and an exchange no earthly banker can reckon. This is an exchange of weakness for weakness. The Son empties himself, lets go of his "riches," in order that we who are weak and destitute can receive him without indignity or judgment. Only the most frozen of souls can be free from the vulnerability relationship demands. Thus, if we allow the Lord of Life to draw near, we shall find that our poverty is no longer impoverished and our weaknesses no longer weak, for God himself comes to earth to defeat death by surrender and the powers of hell with the emptiness of the Crucified One.

This dynamic of exchanging God's weakness for our strength provides an insight into what it is that Jesus asks of us when he asks us to follow him by denying ourselves. This is not some maniacal call to self-harm; it is the humble invitation to realize truly that there are still parts of ourselves that do not yet want to belong to Jesus. There are parts of us where we still prefer the "power" of autonomy—the sins of the dark, the secret thoughts that reduce others to mere irritants, the blasphemies we utter under our breath—over the risks of relationship. Letting another lead us, that is, allowing another to matter to us, is to risk both conversion as well as heartache.

But it is only here that we finally learn the truth of what it means to lose our life. In an orthodox teaching of deification, men and women are asked to die to their false selves, those parts of each of our hearts that hold on to ourselves in fear and mistrust of God's will. We have to crucify those sinful desires that keep us from being able to receive the fullness of Christ as he longs to pour himself into all recesses of our souls and throughout every aspect of our lives. Or as a young Joseph Ratzinger (Pope Emeritus Benedict XVI) once wrote, "This exchange consists of God taking upon himself our human existence in order to bestow his divine existence upon us, of his choosing our nothingness in order to give us his plenitude."[3] This is why the Son chooses to save us as he does: to lose in earthly death so that we could prevail in eternal life.

Divine Adoption and Co-Heirs with Christ

Because of the Son's descent into the human condition, all of humanity has been changed forever. The God-made-human is now able to dwell personally in any other human soul humble enough to allow him entry. When this happens, the sinful tendencies of that man or woman are transformed, their desires are consecrated, and they are

---

[3] Joseph Ratzinger, "Three Meditations on Christmas," in *Dogma and Preaching: Applying Christian Doctrine to Daily Life* (San Francisco: Ignatius Press, 2011), 332.

each made children of the same heavenly Father and Immaculate Mother. The Scriptures are quite adamant that a way of describing this incorporation is through the familial imagery of adoption.

It is true that, by nature, God the Father has only one begotten Son. This Son becomes the man Jesus Christ through the surrender of Mary, the perfect woman from Nazareth. In so doing, he has assumed all of humanity into this same network of loving relationships. For in Christ, the Christian, too, becomes an adopted child of God, a child of Mary. St. Paul uses the term "adoption" five times in his letters (Gal 4:5; Rom 8:15, 23; Rom 9:4; Eph 1:5), encouraging the first Christians to see their new life no longer in only political or juridical terms, but in terms of family life, where they are desired and now accepted into a network of security and love that can never be undone.

This must have been somewhat of a shock to those reading his words because adoption was not a common practice among the ancient Israelites. In pagan societies, a form of adoption was the way of securing ties and building important alliances. But one must be born into a Jewish family where blood lineage is so essential to one's identity as a member of the covenant. This, then, is obviously something novel with the New Covenant in Christ. Before the Incarnation, God could only love and father us from above; now in his Incarnate Son, who has become human for our sake, the Father is able to incorporate us into his own Son's Body.

In so doing, the God-made-flesh is now able to form his own life within the souls of his faithful (Gal 4:19) and thereby adopt us into his own filiality (Rom 8:14–23) before God the Father and Mary our Mother. To understand the bond God intends in this adoption, think of a human family who has adopted children. Three points are worth considering here. The first is to recognize that the adopted children have become sons and daughters, brothers and sisters, of a new family not out of anything they themselves achieved. They were adopted not, say, because the won the orphanage spelling bee. They were adopted out of the love a father and mother manifested for them. We are Christians not out of any merit or achievement of our own; we are brothers and sisters of Christ and all the saints because God our Father and Mary our Mother have brought us into their own love out of nothing other than their love. The Christian faith is pure gift, offered to all out of the Father's love for the human race into which he sends his own beloved Son. One Son by nature was not enough for this prodigal Father, who wanted countless sons and daughters, so through the grace of adoption, he brings mortal sinners into his own Triune Life.

The second dynamic of adoption to consider is how ignoble we would consider human parents who would discriminate between their naturally born and their adopted children. How unworthy of the names "mom and dad" they would be if they treated their biological children somehow better than their adopted kids. If that is true for us sinners, how true is it that God our Father and Mary our Mother do not discriminate between us, their adopted children, and Jesus Christ, the only-begotten Son? Is it true? Does God love us just as much as he loves Jesus? The DNA might be different, how we are God's children may differ, but the reality is the same: Jesus is Son by nature; we, children by grace, yet the love of God and the intercessory care of Our Lady are the same: infinite and incessant.

The third dynamic to consider is the tighter intimacy of divine adoption than of the human family we have been using as our analogy. As beautiful and as laudatory as human adoption is, the parents remain ever outside of their new son or daughter. It is an arrangement juridical and transformative, but one that does remain outward and juridical. Divine adoption, on the other hand, literally transforms us from within because at Baptism, the Divine Life has been planted within us. This infusion of sanctifying grace is nothing other than the presence of the Holy Spirit personally indwelling in those now made sons and daughters of God the Father. It is an adoption not determined by externals but from within, through the actual implantation of divinity within each of us.

It is really the Apostle John who first saw all of this so clearly. He was the youngest, and he was known as "the beloved," so perhaps it's not that surprising to see him open his Gospel by reminding us that in the Word's descent, we have been given "[the] power to become children of God" (John 1:12). From a cosmic Trinitarian start, the Gospel of John holds two truths always in tension: the Word is God and is with God, but it is also this very same Word whose Incarnation opens up God the Father's life to us as well. For the next twenty chapters, Jesus uses the image of rebirth and divine adoption to teach Nicodemus what true life is (John 3:3–5), he tells us that we are his Father's gifts to him (John 17:24–26), and he rejoices in telling Mary Magdalene that he is ascending to their one God and their one Father.

Notice the wording in that beautiful Resurrection scene. After coming to terms with the fact that the one she went out to anoint is now alive, that tremendous lover Mary Magdalene cannot help but rush to embrace her Lord. Now on eternal mission, however, Jesus asks her to let go and instead go into the city and inform the Apostles of what she has witnessed: "Stop holding on to me, for I have not yet ascended to the Father. But go to my brothers and tell them, 'I am going to my Father and your Father, to my God and your God'" (John 20:17). The purpose and end of each human life is this "ascending to the Father," but how we call upon him and how we approach him is here distinguished. Christ is going to the One who is his Father by nature and who is our Father by grace; he is ascending to the One with whom he is God consubstantially and who is our God through participation. Same Father, same God, but in Christ's and our lives in essentially different ways.

This distinction is real and necessary. Even in the most robust theologies of deification, we could never become divine the way Jesus Christ is divine. His divinity is eternally inherent, and ours is a graced invitation to partake of a reality which is never presumed, deserved, or ours apart from its being forever a gift. To think otherwise is to commit the blasphemy and the idolatry of self-divinization. But as we can detect from the initial act of creation itself, the God revealed in Sacred Scripture is never greedy nor selfish. He longs to lavish, and in Christ, we see a Son who is more than willing, who will even die to do so, to share his Father and his Blessed Mother with others. This assimilation of the Christian into Christ comes through in so many ways in Scripture. Let us now therefore turn to the third image we find in the Gospels and in the Epistles: Christians being conformed to the Person of Jesus Christ so as to live and act like Christ himself.

Divine Conformity

The Beloved Apostle John was made intimately aware that this human journey we are all on is ordered to its proper destiny in Christ. John is the one who stresses that the inequality between God and humans is washed away in the Incarnation. Whereas before, the divine and the human were at odds and only a servile relationship could be established, in the God-made-man, man and God can now become friends, other selves: "I no longer call you slaves, . . . I have called you friends" (John 15:15). The dissonance between the perfect and the broken is overcome in the Son's descent into the human condition. Pre-Christian thinkers like Aristotle and Cicero defined a friend as "another self" who most intimately and accurately reflects what it is we most truly cherish in ourselves. We are drawn to our friends because they share our loves and help dispel our fears; they point out to us with another set of eyes what we find most beautiful and offer us another heart to share with us what we hold most dear.

C. S. Lewis, whose presentation of becoming "little Christs" we examine in chapter 7, once wrote that friendship begins when we can look at another in all honesty and exclaim, "Oh, you too?" It is this sharing of selves, this sharing of loves that establishes the Incarnation: The Father "so loved the world that he gave his only Son" (John 3:16) and, in response, we should love God so much that we strive to become like his Son. This is a conformity we all know that may begin now but will be complete only in heaven. For there we shall receive God as fully as a creature can and then not only rejoice, but become like him for all eternity: "Beloved, we are God's children now; what we shall be has not yet been revealed. We do know that when it is revealed we shall be like him, for we shall see him as he is" (1 John 3:2). Here St. John combines two images of deification: the more standard metaphor of divine adoption along with the goal of becoming like God. What is intriguing here is how that final end happens: knowing God by seeing him as he is.

Accordingly, when we are finally conformed to Christ, living heavenly lives, partially even here and now, we can begin to live Jesus's life, having allowed him to live ours. This means that we can do super-human things, like pray for those who persecute us and love our enemies, but even the greater acts like those outlined in the Sermon on the Mount—to thirst and hunger for righteousness, to become poor in spirit, to rejoice at insults and contempt for the name of Christ, to be pure in heart, and to long for a new heaven and new earth (see Matt 5:1–12).

Modern Christians can too easily forget about the height of this call: we are urged by God himself to become like him through surrender and subsequent union. It is telling that the *Catechism of the Catholic Church* opens by instructing us that God's desire is to bring us all into union with himself. The opening words of the most magisterial of Catholic teachings today begins not with a proposition but with a person, a divine Person, or better with the Trinity of Blessedness which God wills to share with other persons. Eternal life is therefore not simply some state of being, some promised land, but a relationship with the One who alone can satisfy all our hungers, soothe all our unrests. The goal of the Christian life described here is then to know this loving Person and those in union with him, his Son Jesus Christ and his Holy Spirit.

> God, infinitely perfect and blessed in himself, in a plan of sheer goodness freely created man to make him share in his own blessed life. For this reason, at every time and in every place, God draws close to man. He calls man to seek him, to know him, to love him with all his strength. He calls together all men, scattered and divided by sin, into the unity of his family, the Church. To accomplish this, when the fullness of time had come, God sent his Son as Redeemer and Savior. In his Son and through him, he invites men to become, in the Holy Spirit, his adopted children and thus heirs of his blessed life. (CCC §1)

Charity always has the first word: Love is the very essence of God—Lover, Beloved, and the Love who is the Holy Spirit—and love is what drew God to earth to reform sinful men and women into a new family and into a new way of life which is his Church.

This is the story of the *Catechism*, this is the story of all of salvation history, and it must become the story of each of our lives. While God needs nothing outside of himself, he has chosen to bring us not only into existence—for that would be too meager—but even chooses to bring us into his own life. He thus decides that this is most fittingly accomplished by the Son of God becoming the Son of Mary, thereby elevating the entire human family into the same divine community. Relying on the major insights of Vatican II's *Lumen Gentium* (quoting §2 three times here), the *Catechism* goes on to teach that:

> "The eternal Father, in accordance with the utterly gratuitous and mysterious design of his wisdom and goodness, created the whole universe and chose to raise up men to share in his own divine life," to which he calls all men in his Son. "The Father . . . determined to call together in a holy Church those who should believe in Christ." This "family of God" is gradually formed and takes shape during the stages of human history, in keeping with the Father's plan. In fact, "already present in figure at the beginning of the world, this Church was prepared in marvelous fashion in the history of the people of Israel and the old Alliance. Established in this last age of the world and made manifest in the outpouring of the Spirit, it will be brought to glo-

rious completion at the end of time." (CCC §759)

The perfect Trinity of love chooses to be unfurled and, in so doing, freely brings about the goodness of creation and then those made in his own image and likeness. This creative love forms first the chosen people of Israel and through them continues to unfold into the one and holy, apostolic Church and will continue to expand from there until the end of created time.

As such, the Lord provides every possible means he can to attract us out of our self-imposed selfishness and into himself. He first gave us the beauty of creation, but we misused that, placing what our eyes desired over what our hearts were instructed to do. We then received the Law and the Prophets, but they, too, proved insufficient. Finally, God himself chose to enter his own creation personally and physically.

Always true to his promise, this enfleshed God continues to make present his own divine presence. This is the Church, and this is what the *Catechism* outlines: Section One on what it is the Church believes (creed), Section Two on how the Church sacramentally praises God (celebration), Section Three on how members of the Church are to live holy lives (conduct), and Section Four on how Christians are invited to pray furthermore into God's own life (communion). But nowhere is this theology of deification more evident than in the four reasons the Church provides when answering why it is the Word became flesh.

The first answer is obvious enough in this fallen world: the Son of God became a man in order to reconcile men and women back to God (CCC §457). The second reason is that we might come to know the extent—the unlimited extent—of God's love for us (CCC §458), while §459 teaches that God took on flesh in order to be our model of holiness and thus provide the way we all need for our own eternal wholeness. But the fourth and final reason (CCC §460) proves to be the crescendo of what motivated God's Incarnation, relying on the best of the Church's apostles and theologians:

> The Word became flesh to make us "partakers of the divine nature" (2 Pet 1:4): "For this is why the Word became man, and the Son of God became the Son of man: so that man, by entering into communion with the Word and thus receiving divine sonship, might become a son [or daughter] of God" (St. Irenaeus [d. ca. 200]). "For the Son of God became man so that we might become God" (St. Athanasius of Alexandria [d. 373]). "The only-begotten Son of God, wanting to make us sharers in his divinity, assumed our nature, so that he, made man, might make men gods" (St. Thomas Aquinas, O.P. [d. 1274]).

Could there be a clearer window into what Christianity is all about? Could there be more joyous news that God became like us so we could become like him? This is the Gospel, this is the Church's entire mission: to preach the power of Jesus Christ to transform us from sinners into saints, from strangers and sojourners into co-heirs and children of the same heavenly Father and mother.

·✦·

CHAPTER 4

Who Do You Say That I Am?
(Matt 16:15)

You might have noticed that these pages are dedicated
to Rita and Michael Mooney. This fun-loving couple
are faithful Catholics and dear friends who stopped by
my office one day here at the Catholic Studies Centre
at St. Louis University as I was writing these pages. As
we talked, Mike asked what I thought about—what he
called—"The most important words in Scripture: 'But
who do you say that I am?'" (Matt 16:15). *Hmm, the most
important?* I wondered. Perhaps so, for it is this question
that every human soul must answer. It is this question that
determines not only how we live these decades on earth
but where and how we shall spend eternity as well.

As such, this chapter focuses in on the indispensable
beginning of humanity's attaining our ultimate end, the
Incarnation. Who does the Church say that Jesus Christ
is, and how does the manner of his Incarnation effect our

salvation? This is a question the first ecumenical councils of the Church sought to answer, and the question which centuries of theology have tried to clarify more and more articulately throughout the ages. It is a question that has a direct bearing on our attempt in this book to present the Christian life as a life of deifying transformation because only a God-made-human can make humans gods.

To answer the Mooneys' query, this chapter proceeds by way of the Church's answer to Christ's own question. Who do we, in fact, say he is? The answer it took some time to formulate is the Church's magisterial insight that Jesus Christ is a divine Person dwelling now and eternally in two distinct natures, both fully divine and fully human. How we got to this answer will be the first half of this chapter while the second half will lay out what this Christological truth has to do with our lives in Christ and how he continues his own Incarnation in and through each of us.

God loves us so much he wanted to become like us. Is that not what love does: unites the lover with his or her beloved, making them to some degree "one"? In humanity, God saw his own unique handiwork suffering and dying, and he could not let them wander, and so he took to himself those whom he loves, those for whom he was willing to die. "Christ wanted to be what we are so that we could become what Christ is."[1] Our withering flesh, our gray-

---

[1] St. Cyprian of Carthage, *On the Vanity of Idols*, §11.

ing hair, our mortal bodies did not scare the perfect God away. In fact, it was our own limitations that endeared us to him so that he offered us an exchange of his own perfection: "He clothed himself with our course materiality, that I might become God just as much as he became a man."[2] This is who God is; this is what Christianity is: a "two act play" wherein God first becomes human in order that we humans can then become godly. This is why God becomes a man, and this is what the Church is divinely commissioned to teach.

The Church's Answer: Fully God, Fully Man

So, who does the Church say Jesus is? The Scriptures are, of course, the ultimate source to answer this question, but those divinely inspired pages must be read correctly. There we read about this miraculous conception of a new kind of ruler (see Luke 1:32–33), and we are brought into the supernormal events surrounding the birth of this baby Jesus (see Matt 2). We then read of the miracles and sayings of this carpenter's Son, who suggests that his presence on earth has now somehow inaugurated the true kingdom of God (see Matt 3:2, 4:17; Mark 1:15). But does Jesus anywhere tell us who he truly is? He drops hints, he makes suggestions, but as is the way of Love, he always elicits our desires and never uses his divine irrefutability to force our

---

[2] Gregory of Nazianzus, *Oration* 40.45.

assent. So, "Who do you say that I am?"

Why isn't Jesus clearer about his true identity? Well, could anyone really prove who they are by providing definitions or handing out a sheet with bullet points listing their personal characteristics? Would we not all think, *This is precisely the kind of definition an imposter—or a crazy man—would afford himself?* While we might want more clarity from the Bible, is that the way any of our truly lovely relationships developed? Of course not. We come to know, love, and trust another by spending time with that person, coming to realize his or her uniqueness, and experiencing the care this person has for each of us in return.

In the two thousand-year-long answer of "Who do you say that I am?," there have been many heretics who have unduly stressed one of Jesus's natures at the cost of the other. Early on, there was a group of Christians known as the Docetists who stressed Christ's divinity to the point that he only *seemed* human (from the Greek verb *dokeo* meaning "to appear"). Other groups took some of Jesus's sayings like, "Why do you call me good? No one is good but God alone" (Mark 10:18) or that "the Father is greater than I" (John 14:28) to mean that Jesus was not really, truly God (not "consubstantial") but some sort of lower deity of a lesser substance or nature. Such misleading interpretations of the Bible have led to great confusion, especially during the early centuries of the Church's life. In turn, the Church continued to follow the example of the first Apostles at the Council of Jerusalem (Acts 15) and convene sacred synods to address problems, correct heresies, and purify doctrine.

Surprisingly, the first official convocation of bishops from all over the known world came through an unbaptized emperor who was probably more worried about the unity of a large percentage of his people than he was about doctrinal orthodoxy. In the year AD 325, Emperor Constantine (d. 337) convened the first ecumenical council of the Church in a small city outside his residence in Constantinople in modern-day Turkey—Nicaea by name. Here in the spring of 325 about 318 Churchmen gathered to decide how best to clarify the relationship between God the Father and God the Son. These deliberations are still on the lips of God's people, as every Sunday and on more festive Christian celebrations, the Church proclaims that Jesus really is

the Only Begotten Son of God, born of the Father before all ages. God from God, Light from Light, true God from true God, begotten, not made, consubstantial with the Father; through him all things were made. For us men and for our salvation he came down from heaven, and by the Holy Spirit was incarnate of the Virgin Mary, and became man. For our sake he was crucified under Pontius Pilate, he suffered death and was buried, and rose again on the third day in accordance with the Scriptures. He ascended into heaven and is seated at the right hand of the Father. He will come again in glory to judge the living and the dead and his kingdom will have no end.

In this middle section of the Nicene Creed, Christians are asked to place their faith in One who is eternally begotten from the Father and therefore equal in dignity and in divinity.

Just as human parents eventually beget human children (albeit in time), the Creed shows how God the Father begets one divine Child, his Son, not in time but "before all ages." This is an eternal begetting, a timeless coming forth, as there was never a time when the First Person of the Trinity was not Father, and never was there a time without the Son (and the Holy Spirit). As we saw back in chapter 2, Divine Fatherhood is an eternal state of being for the First Person of the Trinity, wholly dependent upon his Son to be who he is as Father. As his Fatherhood is forever simultaneous with the First Person of the Trinity, so is Sonship the primal and unshakeable definition of what it means to be Son. Yet, "when the fullness of time had come" (Gal 4:4), "for us" and for "our salvation," this divine Son took on the fullness of the human condition through the free allowance of the Blessed Mother.

In uniting his divine Personhood to our human nature,

the Son—now named Jesus and known as the Christ (the Messiah, the Anointed One)—now lives as both God and human. He has freely chosen to take on all that we are. As St. Paul says, he has "emptied" himself of his divinity (Phil 2:7), meaning that he did not forfeit his divine Sonship but has chosen to live his godliness through and as a mere man among men. Think of it this way: in the Lord Jesus Christ, God did not save the world from heaven but from earth; he saved the world not by remaining God but by becoming human; he redeemed humankind not through strength and domination but by weakness and the Cross. This is utter humility, to take on a nature and a fate not your own. In so doing, God has elevated the entire human race, every man, woman, and child, into his own Divine Life. At the Incarnation of the Christ, it is not God who changes, but it is we who have been renewed.

When I speak a word, it is not the invisible word in my mind that changes. Instead, it is the stuff I "add" to that mental word in order to make it audible in the external world. What changes when I speak is not so much the word springing from my brain, but it is the air and the spit, the tooth and the tongue, that I use to make that word heard by those near me. In the same way, when the Son—the Word—became human, it was not he who changed, but it was all the "stuff" he assumed to himself in order to make his otherwise invisible and inaudible self, known to the world of space and time. What changed was not God but human—human flesh, the human mind, passions, and emotions, all that make us who we are.

As the Church's teaching on Christ developed, exactly how these two natures of our Lord—divine and human—interacted with each other had to be addressed. While the first ecumenical Council of Nicaea in 325 had to address the heresiarch Arius' claim that the Son must be a bit less than the Father, otherwise there would be two gods, the fourth ecumenical Council of Chalcedon in 451 set out to address the two natures of this one divine Person who lived, died, and rose from the dead for our sake. The Council of Chalcedon was in response to another heretic, the powerful and influential monk Eutyches, who was successful in teaching that the truth of our salvation lay in the fact that the Son's Divine Nature actually absorbed his human nature and was now, in fact, only one real nature. This heresy was known as Monophysitism, as it claimed the Lord was only one (*mono*) nature (*physis*) and that his humanity was of no avail now that God and man had become one.

During this time, the See of Peter was filled by one of the great minds of the early Church, Pope Leo the Great (440–61). Pope St. Leo was a masterful administrator and quite a prayerful theologian. He knew how Eutyches' Monophysitism was not the way God has chosen to save us. God has chosen to need our humanity, and instead of destroying it, he has chosen to deify it. The humanity of Christ is essential in uniting our humanity to the only true source of salvation. It is the nexus between God and human persons.

This is the Catholic Tradition in a nutshell: The flesh of Christ is "the hinge of salvation"[3] (*caro cardo salutis*); "If it is not assumed it is not redeemed, in Christ";[4] and "You didn't have anything to live by, and he didn't have anything to die with. What a marvelous exchange [*o magna mutatio*]. Live by what is his because he died with what is yours."[5] Continuing this great symphony, Pope St. Leo offered a most beautiful Christology, contained in a letter to Bishop Flavian of Constantinople, who presided over the Council of Chalcedon, now known as Pope St. Leo's *Tome*. In Pope St. Leo's Christology, the faithful are brought into the interplay between divinity and humanity in the most illuminative pieces of early Christian thought on the person of Jesus Christ:

> Accordingly while the distinctness of both natures and substances was preserved, and both meet in one Person, lowliness is assumed by majesty,

---

[3] Tertullian, *On the Resurrection of the Flesh*, §8.

[4] Gregory of Nazianzen, *Epistle* 101, his letter critiquing the heresy of Apollinarianism which wrongly taught the divine Logos replaced the human mind in Jesus Christ.

[5] Augustine, *Sermon* 265D.

weakness by power, mortality by eternity; and in order to pay the debt of our condition, the inviolable nature was united to the passible, so that, as the appropriate remedy for our ills, one and the same "Mediator between God and men, the man Christ Jesus," might from one element be capable of dying, and from the other be incapable. Therefore in the entire and perfect nature of very Man was born very God, whole in what was his, whole in what was ours.[6]

Pope St. Leo laid the groundwork for our understanding that the two natures of Jesus are always distinct but never separate, acting in unison but never mixed with the other. Jesus Christ is fully God and fully human, he is thus eternally "consubstantial" with God his Father as well as "consubstantial" with Mary his Mother, as he is conceived in her womb as a divine Person now dwelling wholly and completely as one of us.

In being fully human—"entire and perfect nature of very man," as St. Leo writes here—Jesus appears as the New Adam who, before sin, was the fullness of the human race. St. Leo realized the implications of this image of Christ as the New Adam, as St. Paul first laid it out at

---

[6] Pope Leo's *Tome* (Epistle to Flavian), in *Christology of the Later Fathers*, ed. Edward Hardy (Louisville: Westminster John Knox Press [1953] 2006), 363, §3.

Romans 5:12–21, describing sin entering the human race through one man and, thankfully, grace and the redemption of our sins coming through one Man as well. This is the New Man who takes on "sinful flesh" by condemning sin as One also in human flesh (Rom 8:3). As followers of an incarnate God, we must always remember that the Scriptures use "flesh" as a shorthand term *not* for the badness of the human body, of course, but for our fallen desires after we turned away from the One who made us body and soul. That is why the Church has never refrained from emphasizing the glorious flesh of our Savior: while eternally being one in essence with the Father, the Son has now become one with his mother's humanity, thereby redeeming humanity as God-made-human:

> For if the New Man had not been made in the likeness of sinful flesh, and taken on Him our old nature, and being consubstantial with the Father, had deigned to be consubstantial with His mother also, and being alone free from sin, had united our nature to Him the whole human race would be held in bondage beneath the Devil's yoke, and we should not be able to make use of the Conqueror's victory, if it had been won outside our nature.

> But from Christ's marvelous sharing of the two natures, the mystery of regeneration shone upon

us that through the self-same spirit, through whom Christ was conceived and born, we too, who were born through the desire of the flesh, might be born again from a spiritual source: and consequently, the Evangelist speaks of believers as those "who were born not of blood, nor of the will of the flesh, nor of the will of man, but of God" (see John 1:13). And of this unutterable grace no one is a partaker, nor can be reckoned among the adopted sons of God, who excludes from his faith that which is the chief means of our salvation.[7]

By taking fullness of human nature to himself in the womb of the Blessed Virgin, Christ has thereby united divinity to all of humanity, now regathered in this new covenant effected by God's becoming flesh. The totality of the Father is eternally present in Christ insofar as he is God; the whole of who we are is now present in Christ insofar as he is human.

This is why Christians bear the name of the Christ and not explicitly the name of God the Father or of the Holy Spirit. It is the God who has become human who alone offers humans the godliness for which we were

---

[7] Pope Leo, *Epistle* 31.2–3, in *Nicene and Post-Nicene Fathers*, trans. Charles Feltoe (Peabody, MA: Hendrickson Publishers [1894] 2004) 45. This letter is to the Empress Pulcheria, whose support against the heresiarch Eutyches the pope is soliciting.

originally created. It is the flesh of Christ the Son which makes us all sons and daughters of the same Father and mother. This remains the Church's ultimate message, evidenced so early on in her life:

> The Father of immortality sent his immortal Son and Word into the world. . . . To give us a new birth that would make our bodies and souls immortal, he breathed into us the spirit of life and armed us with incorruptibility. Now if we become immortal, we shall also be divine; and if we become divine after rebirth in baptism through water and the Holy Spirit, we shall also be coheirs with Christ after the resurrection of the dead. . . . Whoever goes down into these waters of rebirth with faith renounces the devil and pledges himself to Christ. He repudiates the enemy and confesses that Christ is God, throws off his servitude, and is raised to filial status.[8]

Because of this divinely-desired covenant with every human, Jesus tells us to deny ourselves. "Whoever loves his life loses it, and whoever hates his life in this world will preserve it for eternal life" (John 12:25). This is not a call

---

[8] From a sermon on the Epiphany attributed to Hippolytus of Rome (d. 235) as found in the Office of Readings for Epiphany, *The Liturgy of the Hours*, vol. 1 (New York: Catholic Book Publishing Co., 1975), 587.

to destroy that which is eternally precious in the Father's eyes, his very own children, but to get rid of anything that keeps me at the center of my own private world.

If we are made for divine union. We must, therefore, detect what in ourselves keeps us from seeing that the fullness of our life is relational, covenantal, and other-centered, and this center must be found in no creature but in God alone. "Whoever finds his life will lose it, and whoever loses his life for my sake will find it" (Matt 10:39; see also Mark 8:35, Luke 9:24, 17:33). This is why the Great Liberator, the Master of all Freedom, Jesus Christ, tells us to yoke ourselves: "Take my yoke upon you and learn from me, for I am meek and humble of heart; and you will find rest for yourselves" (Matt 11:29). He knows there is no such thing as a yoke-less life: we shall either unite ourselves to God or to the world, to the divine or to the devil.

But this is precisely who our Triune God is: three Persons so "yoked" to one another that their entire identity is found in the other. This same love of unity is not only how God created outside of him, but it is precisely how he also wishes to bring us back to him. In his unmatchable way, C. S. Lewis, writing here as the Enemy of our human nature, old Screwtape, contrasts the way God desires union with the alternative way the world offers it:

He really *does* want to fill the universe with a lot of loathsome little replicas of Himself —creatures whose life, on its miniature scale, will be qualitatively like His own, not because He has absorbed them but because their wills freely conform to His. We want cattle who can finally become food; He wants servants who can finally become sons. We want to suck in, He wants to give out. We are empty and would be filled; He is full and flows over. Our war aim is a world in which Our Father Below has drawn all other beings into himself: the Enemy wants a world full of beings united to Him but still distinct.[9]

Once we begin to understand that the Lord is the One who has created us for himself, once we finally realize intensely that the deepest desires of our hearts are actually gifts from our loving, selfless Father, and as we continue to understand the significance of the Incarnation—of finding God in and through the created goods of this world, with love of neighbor supreme—we shall finally feel the stresses and tensions of our mortality, our political anxieties, our economic worries, and so on, placed into our loving Savior's pierced hands, realizing ever more deeply that he has given his very life for our eternal joy.

When Jesus is pressed to clarify if he is living on earth really as the Son of God, the long-awaited Messiah, he

---

[9] C. S. Lewis, *The Screwtape Letters* (San Francisco: Harper Collins, [1942] 2001), 38–39.

uses the beloved Psalms of his Jewish audience to remind them that being a child of the Father is really what this life is all about. Let us recall this lengthier scene from John's Gospel:

> The Jews gathered around him and said to him, "How long are you going to keep us in suspense? If you are the Messiah, tell us plainly."

> Jesus answered them, "I told you and you do not believe. The works I do in my Father's name testify to me. But you do not believe, because you are not among my sheep. My sheep hear my voice; I know them, and they follow me. I give them eternal life, and they shall never perish. No one can take them out of my hand. My Father, who has given them to me, is greater than all, and no one can take them out of the Father's hand. The Father and I are one."

> The Jews again picked up rocks to stone him. Jesus answered them, "I have shown you many good works from my Father. For which of these are you trying to stone me?"

> The Jews answered him, "We are not stoning you for a good work but for blasphemy. You, a man, are making yourself God."

Jesus answered them, "Is it not written in your law, 'I said, "You are gods" (Ps 82:6)'? If it calls them gods to whom the word of God came, and scripture cannot be set aside, can you say that the one whom the Father has consecrated and sent into the world blasphemes because I said, 'I am the Son of God'"? (John 10:24–36)

What a scene! What a lesson! Here is Jesus Christ, the Son of the carpenter, one who looks like every other man around him, saying that he and the One true God in the heavens, the One who established the covenant with their father Abraham, are actually single in being. "The Father and I are one." He then draws deeply into Jewish devotion and reminds his hearers that they, too, can become "gods" by allowing themselves to be consecrated by the same Father. The Sonship of Jesus is not grasped selfishly by him, but it is a manner of life before the Father which the Son longs to share joyfully with everyone else. They simply have to allow themselves to be drawn intimately into the one whose divine presence fulfills our human longings.

Before the Latin phrase *alter Christus* was used in an exclusive way for the priest only, the "other Christ" who sacramentally continues Christ's sacrifice before the Father, it was used for the baptized souls who in the waters of that sacred font have also become one with Christ. *Induimini Christum*, "put on the Lord Jesus Christ," we are instructed by St. Paul (Rom 13:14), and this "putting on Christ" is no mere moral agreement that we shall try to be good. Coming to Christ truly means that we are actually made extended reflections of Jesus's own life in a mystical but real way. "So then you who have become sharers in Christ are appropriately called Christs."[10] "Let us rejoice and give thanks that we have become not only Christians, but Christ himself."[11] It is, therefore, no longer rules that save, as the Law is now of no avail (Rom 7:6; Gal 2:16, 3:24–25). Not rules but relationship; not obedience but union.

This is not to say that Christians are no longer held to a high moral standard. We, of course, are. But our moral lives must come from a deep connection with Christ in our souls, so deep we actually allow him to live our lives, to think our thoughts, to use our eyes and hands, as we begin to live his life each in our own particular way. None of us is strong enough to live a life of integrity, not to mention charity and peace and joy, but Christ and Our Lady are. We simply have to allow them to do that in us:

What the law cannot do, God can and does accomplish. His adoption of us actually confers a divine sonship upon us: *He gave them power to be made the sons of God, to them that believed in him*

[10] Cyril of Jerusalem, *Mystagogical Catecheses* 3.1; quoted in CCC §2782.
[11] Augustine, *Commentary on John* 21.8; quoted in CCC §795.

. . . . Our first parents were tempted to sin by the promise: *You shall be as Gods.* Instead, the sin of Adam and Eve debased man almost to the level of the animals. What sin failed to give man, has been bestowed upon him by divine love, for by the Incarnation God became man so that man might become divine. In the words of Saint Peter: *We are made partakers of the divine nature.* . . . Humanly speaking, it is not possible for us to attain such glory, but by the power of God the impossible is accomplished, for by divine grace man becomes Godlike! We regard the raising of a dead person to life as a stupendous miracle, but such a marvel pales into insignificance compared to the effect sanctifying grace produces in the soul. This bestowal on man of a participation in the divine life of God is God's greatest work, surpassing as it does his creation of the universe.[12]

It takes a while to fathom the meaning of all of this. In the divine humanity of Jesus Christ, every human soul is now united to the Son of God. Every human soul now has the opportunity to live no longer on its own power but to live in and even "as" Christ. The life of the Trinity has been opened up for us, the Divine Nature is now accessi-

---

[12] William Raymond Bonniwell, O.P., *What Think You of Christ?* (St. Louis: Herder Books, 1958), 8–9.

ble through the Second Person of the Trinity who, for our sake, has become fully human. On the Cross he died all of our deaths; from that empty tomb he is now living all of our truest lives—free from sin and death, heavenly and eternal. Yet he waits for our surrender; he waits for each of us to imitate his own Mother and entrust to God these words, "May it be done to me according to your word" (Luke 1:38).

CHAPTER 5

Temples of the Holy Spirit (1 Cor 6:19)

The Dominican Sisters of Mary, Mother of the Eucharist are a new group of consecrated women. After only twenty or so years, they already have about two hundred sisters in their burgeoning order! These women are young, joyful, and filled with the love of Christ and our Blessed Mother. They are fully habited (of course), faithful to Christ's voice in his Church, and are true signs of hope and springtime for the world. While traveling in the South a while back, two of these sisters, with veils and habits blowing in the wind, were walking into a local lunch spot when they caught the attention of a little boy who gazed up at his own mother and said, "Mama, look at those churches."

What does it mean to be a temple, a locus of divine presence? What does it mean to walk around as a "church"? Perhaps there was no more confusing and challenging line to his Jewish brothers and sisters than when Jesus said that the God with whom they were in covenant was not to be found in the Temple of Solomon, which the Jewish people had so devoutly been building up for centuries. Now, however, one of their own teachers was telling them that they were to find the divine presence in their own belovedness before the Father: "Do you not know that you are the temple of God, and that the Spirit of God dwells in you? If anyone destroys God's temple, God will destroy that person; for the temple of God, which you are, is holy" (1 Cor 3:16–17). This is the Church: Christ alive in a sanctified soul. Holiness is God living his life in us, and as we recognize that we have become his sons and daughters, replicas of the Christ, we begin to sense the Spirit alive in our souls. This is usually done by a new buoyancy in life: enjoying created goods only in and for the sake of Christ (saying grace before meals, for example, thanking God for all the goodness which meets us throughout each day—that conversation, that safe arrival to the store, the weather, etc.)—coming to hate our sins more, and looking for ways to strategize so as to grow in virtue and integrity. The Holy Spirit is the One who proves to be that spark of divine love in each of us.

This chapter will examine the role of the Holy Spirit in transforming Christians into Christ. Pondering how most of the Church's saints and theologians depict the Holy Spirit and his effects in their lives, a convenient three-fold "C" pattern came to mind: communion, conviction, and consecration. That is, the first role the Holy Spirit plays in the lives of Christians is that of unifying them with both God and with one another. This communion is essential in our holiness because we are saved by becoming one with Christ, and it is his Spirit who proves to be the bond of charity. The second effect of the Holy Spirit is the purging of sin in our lives, what the Gospels call the conviction of sin. To convict another is the opposite of condemning them; convict means to overcome a fault by pointing it out, which is very different than condemning, which means to damn someone for what they have done. The first is a beginning; the second is the end. Thirdly, the Holy Spirit longs to consecrate our lives. At the moment we are baptized, we are his sacred temples, living dwelling places of the Spirit and, consequently, everything we do and think and say on earth can be for the greater glory of God and our life in the Blessed Trinity, allowing us to live as saints and children of the Father even now.

Communion

Remember how the Holy Spirit is described as the Love between the Lover and the Beloved, the Gift between the Father and the Son—Giver and Receiver, Begetter and Begotten. The Holy Spirit is the glue, the living connection, whose eternal role is that of uniting persons. This is his life in the Trinity, and it is therefore his life in the Church on earth as well. It is the Holy Spirit who unites persons: he unites us with God, he unites his Church into one, and he even is the one who integrates our own faculties so we can live with purity in singularity of mind and heart. In fact, this is a truth we pray often and hear throughout the Holy Mass: "To you Father, through your Son, *in the unity of the Holy Spirit.*" Interpersonal communion is the life of the Holy Spirit within the Trinity, and so it follows that the primary task of the Spirit in salvation history is to unite persons: to bring the faithful into union with God, to unite the Church into one Body, and even to unite individual persons as we each grow in integrity and undividedness in Christ.

The first important Greek religious thinkers instinctively knew that the more one was like the gods in virtue, the better one could know the gods intellectually. It was a Pythagorean adage that "like knows like," and that as one grew in heavenly contemplation, one could more and more easily make sense of the divine. When Christianity came upon the world stage, it never dismissed wisdom but instead argued that charity is what unites us with the one true God who is Love. Assuming the axiom that "like knows like," then, Christian thought maintains that when the Holy Spirit enters the soul at baptism, that soul is made more and more like God. St. Thomas Aquinas put this thought in his typical clear and concise manner:

> The soul is made like to God by grace. Hence for a
> divine person to be sent to anyone by grace, there

must needs be a likening of the soul to the divine person Who is sent, by some gift of grace. Because the Holy Spirit is Love, the soul is assimilated to the Holy Spirit by the gift of charity: hence the mission of the Holy Spirit is according to the mode of charity. Whereas the Son is the Word, not any sort of word, but one Who breathes forth Love. Hence Augustine says (*On the Trinity* 9.10): "The Word we speak of is knowledge with love."[1]

Knowledge with love, that is a shorthand definition of a person fully alive. This is why it is not simply knowledge that sanctifies the soul, as important as knowing the truth is. What saves and brings a creature into heaven is charity, and only the Holy Spirit—who is Charity—can instill that into the mortal soul.

If we only knew the gift that God has given us in the Holy Spirit (see John 4:10)! At baptism, most of us were not even aware of the transformation that was being offered us, for the first supernatural gift God gave us at that moment was his very self: the indwelling of the Holy Spirit personally and truly in the human soul. Theologians describe this gift in terms of the theological virtues (faith, hope, and charity), the Gifts of the Holy Spirit (see Isa 11), as well as the Fruits of the Holy Spirit (see

---

[1] Thomas Aquinas, *Summa Theologiae* I, q. 43, a. 5, response to objection 2.

Gal 5). But in the end, what happened at our baptism was nothing other than the Holy Spirit uniting us to the Son and adopting us into God's family before the Father and, by extension, proclaiming Mary our Mother forever. It is as if the Father is the divine Artisan whose eternal and unparalleled production is his Son, and gazing upon his perfect image (Col 1:15), the Father uses the Holy Spirit to make tiny replicas of his Son in us. As such, the Holy Spirit prolongs the Christ-life in each of us:

> The transforming union is the work of the Holy Spirit, who brings to souls the divine fecundity of the Father. But in this mystical work, as in the divine Incarnation, the Holy Spirit requires the cooperation of the creature; the soul overshadowed by the Holy Spirit guided and moved and made fruitful, so to say, by him, forms Jesus in itself.[2]

As the Spirit formed Jesus in the womb of Mary, uniting heaven and earth, he longs to do the same at every baptism. As mundane and as "simple" as that rite may appear, something incredibly awesome is occurring in that soul.

That is why Baptism is ordered to all the other sacraments: the divine seed planted there must be cleansed through Reconciliation, fed by the Most Holy Eucharist,

---

[2] Luis Martínez, *The Sanctifier* (Boston: Pauline Books [1941] 2003), 41. This classic from the Archbishop of Mexico City remains one of the great expositions on the nature and role of the Holy Spirit.

and finally confirmed by the Christian's more mature "yes" and consequent participation. The Spirit will not continue his work unless freely invited to do more, to complete the face of Christ in each of our souls. That is why the divine communion first effected at baptism may seem somewhat inert until it is put into action through the child's growth in wisdom and in love. God's ways are gentle, often silent and still, waiting on us creatures to realize finally what it is we want to become. The Father has such a desire to replicate his Son in each of us. He gives us his own Spirit, he lets his own Son be sacrificed on the Cross, but in the end, the Father has given to each of us the profound power to let his very own life be freely received by each of us.

The first step in letting this union deepen and conform us to this triune movement of love of the Father's sending the Son to give us his Spirit is the realization that we are utterly unworthy and that the initiative is entirely God's and entirely free. On the existential level, it is a deep awareness that we are in no way deserving of such divine communion; that, by nature, we are dust, but by decree of the supernatural, we have been elevated into heavenly co-heirs and children of God. On the moral level, it is a recognition that we are all sinners, and while deserving of damnation, have been offered eternal life. That is why the Gospels teach that the first movement of the Spirit in the mature soul is to convict it of sin.

Conviction

The Gospels promise that when we move into the Light, we not only become brilliant, but our shadows shine all the clearer: "And when [the Holy Spirit] comes he will convict the world in regard to sin and righteousness and condemnation" (John 16:8). The Holy Spirit led the Christ into the desert to do combat with Satan, the Enemy of our human nature. The Spirit also sends the Great Physician into the heart of any sinner willing to receive him and in so doing, offers us the promise that we need never again be a slave to sin. The word "convict" Jesus uses here he has borrowed from the law courts, a term used when cross-examining the accused, *not* in order to rush to his supposed guilty plea but to help the penitent see the whole of his actions with the desire that he is enabled to see the depth of his need for forgiveness.

That is why Catholics begin the celebration of Christ's Mass with a public recognition that we are all in need of God's mercy: "Lord have mercy, Christ have mercy, Lord have mercy." To the world it must seem ironic, if not totally wrong, that we begin worship by admitting our sinfulness. We stand, week after week, next to those whom we have taken for granted, with whom we have grown angry, and so on, and cry out, "Have mercy." But this is the beginning of intimacy.

Have you ever thought of how the person who knows

the worst things about you is most probably the person who loves you the most? We shall tell everyone all of our "good stuff," but only to an intimate few do we feel free and loved enough to discuss our wounds and shortcomings. The power of this paradox is nothing other than the power of the cross: the places in our lives where we feel strong and self-assured are rarely the places where we meet God, but, on the other hand, the places where we know we need grace and feel totally out of control are usually the places where we allow God and others into our lives. How many times have you said this in your life: "Hey, would you please pray for me? I'm having a really, really . . . good day"? It does not usually work that way. We tend to ask others for help only when we are waiting on that serious medical report, when our marriages are in turmoil, when we are feeling stressed and anxious.

When St. Ignatius of Loyola (d. 1556) asks his retreatants to pray over their sins, he surprisingly asks them to pray for the grace of feeling confused: "Pray for the following grace: shame and confusion before God as I consider the effects of sin in my life, my community, and my world."[3] When I was a Jesuit novice, I asked my spiritual director what in the world St. Ignatius could mean by "the graces of shame and confusion." He gave me an a very delicate but powerful image: "Imagine you are driv-

---

[3] Ignatius of Loyola, *Spiritual Exercises*, §48.

ing home and inadvertently swerve over the yellow line," he said. "Now, see the car you mangled, the young driver who might be fatally injured, the sirens, and all the commotion. Now imagine another car pulling up," he slowed. "Here are this child's parents. They get out of their car and walk up to you. They embrace you and say, 'It's okay. We know you didn't mean to do this.'" That's the shame and confusion St. Ignatius wants us to experience when we think about what we have done to God, and if we could only see the full effects of our sin, we would sob endlessly. This is the task of the Holy Spirit: to elicit those tears, to raise that sense of shame and confusion, all the while also confirming us in the love and the absolving embrace of Christ. We have sinned, and we do deserve punishment, but our guilt and insecurities, our sins and our half-heartedness were all nailed to the Cross and slain there through the love of Jesus: "Hence, now there is no condemnation for those who are in Christ Jesus" (Rom 8:1).

Condemnation looks at our past and mocks us of our sins; conviction looks forward with the promise that we need never live like that again. Condemnation tells us our belovedness before God depends on our actions and clear consciences; conviction tells us that God loves us not because we are always loveable but because he is Love and accepts us where we are at any moment we turn to him. God does not punish us for our sins; we are punished by our sins. It is those freely chosen actions which leave us empty and ashamed. In Matthew 13, Jesus provides an amazing image of his patient power to heal. Here he talks about weeds being planted by the Enemy in the garden of each of our life's stories, and in our own zeal to be perfect—what convert or "revert" can't relate?—we think we have to go make ourselves clean, and then we shall be presentable to the Lord. Yet here is what Jesus suggests:

> "An enemy has done this." His slaves said to him, "Do you want us to go and pull them up?" He replied, "No, if you pull up the weeds you might uproot the wheat along with them. Let them grow together until harvest; then at harvest time I will say to the harvesters, "First collect the weeds and tie them in bundles for burning; but gather the wheat into my barn." (Matt 13:28–30)

The Spirit of conversion is slow. He is silent and often noticeable only when we look at our lives backward. In Christ that same Spirit gently moves us and is more patient with our stumbles and scars than we are.

In John's Gospel we receive another image of the paradoxical power of sin in the lives of a follower of Jesus. This time we hear of a man who has been confined to a mat for thirty-eight years. Because of the utter and ugly selfishness of those who rush headlong into those healing waters and leave that poor invalid lying there unattended for decades, he has not been able to be plunged into the restorative waters of Bethesda.

> When Jesus saw him lying there and knew that he had been ill for a long time, he said to him, "Do you want to be well?" The sick man answered him, "Sir, I have no one to put me into the pool when the water is stirred up; while I am on my way, someone else gets down there before me." Jesus said to him, "Rise, take up your mat, and walk." Immediately the man became well, took up his mat, and walked.

> Now that day was a sabbath. So the Jews said to the man who was cured, "It is the sabbath, and it is not lawful for you to carry your mat." He answered them, "The man who made me well told me, 'Take up your mat and walk.'" They asked him, "Who is the man who told you, 'Take it up and walk'?" The man who was healed did not know who it was, for Jesus had slipped away, since there was a crowd there. After this Jesus found him in the temple area and said to him, "Look, you are well; do not sin any more, so that nothing worse may happen to you." The man went and told the Jews that Jesus was the one who had made him well. (John 5:6–15)

The one thing that reminded this man daily that he was an outcast, the one thing he surely prayed day and night to be rid of, the one thing that attached him to the ground from which he could not lift himself—that mat—is the one thing Jesus asks him to continue to carry: "Take up your mat." Normal physicians do not ask their patients to take their gauze or their stitches or even their crutches home, but with Christ, there is no normal healing.

Yet the mat is the one thing that allows others to inquire about this man's healing. It is the one thing that allows the man to evangelize, to tell the world that it was the Christ who healed him. Similar to Christ's own wounds that did not heal after the Resurrection, the sharing of God's power to heal brings joy: "When he had said this, he showed them his hands and his side. *The disciples rejoiced* when they saw the Lord" (John 20:20). Are there not wounds and proverbial "mats" in our lives that we would rather discard and forget about? Are there not experiences and sins that we would simply rather not carry? Perhaps that is why we do not go too deeply into our souls, content with distractions and doing the spiritually minimal. But with Jesus, perhaps those mats and unfortunate moments have been used all along to keep us more merciful with others who also struggle, maybe they have kept us less judgmental and arrogant than if they had never occurred at all.

Notice the stages implicit in this Gospel account:

the man is cleansed, he learns it was Jesus who healed him, and then he goes out in the power of Christ to announce the good news. The early Church Fathers saw in the Christian life a similar three-fold pattern which they called the purgative, the illuminative, and then the unitive stages. Today, the *Catechism* makes clear that the *purgative stage* of the Spirit's presence in our lives is only the beginning. After we surrender to Christ—either through the promises of baptism or through our more adult conscious "yes"—dying to sin is only the first step of our growth in holiness. Next comes what spiritual masters call the *illuminative stage*, that time we begin to learn more about Jesus, study the Faith, and so on. Then comes the *unitive stage* when we finally come to realize that our lives must be spent in Christ, sharing in his riches and ability to fulfill our restless hearts:

> Through the power of the Holy Spirit we take part in Christ's Passion by dying to sin, and in his Resurrection by being born to a new life; we are members of his Body which is the Church, branches grafted onto the vine which is himself: "[God] gave himself to us through his Spirit. By the participation of the Spirit, we become communicants in the divine nature. . . . For this reason, those in whom the Spirit dwells are divinized" (St. Athanasius). (CCC §1988)

The presence of the Spirit in the souls of the divinized is no less "real" than the "Real Presence" of the Son in the Most Blessed Sacrament. The Spirit is thus the one who unites Christ's Body across the world into one Church; the Spirit is thus the one who makes the believer a new tabernacle, a living monstrance in and for the world.

Consecration

This insight should, at one and the same time, bring us unmatchable consolation as well as a certain dread or fear. How easily we let the living Spirit within us know death and decay. But how much more, infinitely more, is the Spirit closer than our sins and more faithful than our own infidelities. That is why in the spiritual masters, the consecration of the soul is the consummate action of the Holy Spirit within the thirsty soul: "Like the traveler pitching his tent in the desert, the Holy Spirit takes possession of souls as their most sweet Guest. But unlike the traveler, who folds his tent as morning breaks, the eternal Guest stays on."[4] The indwelling of the Holy Spirit within the soul is what St. Paul calls becoming spirit, not in the sense of getting rid of our corporeality, but in the sense that the Holy Spirit is the lens through whom we do all things, the metric by which we value all things, the gauge in whom we discern true growth, and so on.

---

[4] Martínez, *The Sancitfier*, 51.

This is St. Paul's "heavenly man" (1 Cor 15:47–49) whom we too shall become as we persevere in appropriating the Christ-life. The ancient Church Father, Cyril of Alexandria (d. 444), who was so pivotal in defending Mary's being rightly called the "Mother of God," points us to the role of the Holy Spirit in our communion with Christ. As we are broken and distorted images of the Trinity, the Son is the perfect fullness of God's own image (Col 1:15), and we need the Spirit to bring us into union with that perfect humanity of Jesus:

> The image of the heavenly man, Christ, is conspicuous in cleanness and purity, in total incorruption and life and sanctification. . . . Union with God is impossible for anyone except through participation in the Holy Spirit, instilling in us His own proper sanctification and refashioning to His own life the nature that fell subject to corruption, and thus restoring to God and to God's likeness what had been deprived of this glory. For the perfect image of the Father is the Son, and the natural likeness of the Son is His Spirit. The Spirit, therefore, refashioning as it were to Himself the souls of men, engraves on them God's likeness and seals the representation of the supreme essence."[5]

---

[5] Cyril of Alexandria, *Commentary on John*, 11.11.

The resurrected humanity of Jesus Christ is thus the key-hole through which the Spirit comes to us: "But I tell you the truth, it is better for you that I go. For if I do not go, the Advocate will not come to you. But if I go, I will send him to you" (John 16:7). In sending us the Spirit, Jesus continues to form his Body on earth, his Mystical Body. In this grafting of us branches onto the perfect Vine, we are finally empowered to bear fruit that will last. This does not mean we are taken out of the world but sent back to our daily routines, only now with a vigor and a joy, knowing that all the seemingly mundane acts asked of us each day can be filled with God's glory by incessantly conversing with the Spirit in our souls, thanking him for each moment's blessings and offering to him all of our intentions and fears and desires.

When the Divine Life is reproduced in us, our lives change. We first begin to realize how silly we have been, thinking for most of our lives that we have been bothering our heavenly Father, or worse, that he is disappointed in us. It is a dogma of Christ's own Church that at Baptism, we have received a share in God's own life, and here we learn how much the Persons of the Trinity love us, are obsessed with us, are thrilled to have us as his own: "For the LORD takes delight in his people" (Ps 149:4). The prophet even described this delight in terms of a spousal union, God's love lifting us out of our sins and doubt and making each of us his own: "No more shall you be called 'Forsaken,' nor your land called 'Desolate,' but you shall be called 'My Delight is in her,' and your land 'Espoused.' For the Lord delights in you, and your land shall be espoused. For as a young man marries a virgin, your Builder shall marry you; And as a bridegroom rejoices in his bride so shall your God rejoice in you" (Isa 62:4–5).

This consecration also brings about a great consolation in this life, the confidence that even now we can trust the Spirit's promise of our going to heaven and thus finally enjoying God fully and eternally. That is, the Spirit's gift of fortitude effects a consecrated trust in our souls that we are destined for heaven. St. Thomas Aquinas, for instance, understands that since the ultimate end or purpose of human life is to be deified and thus one with the divine, we have to receive both the means as well as the conviction of that end from a supernatural Source, namely the Holy Spirit. When that happens, we can trust that despite how broken or unsure we are about things, the Spirit will accomplish in us the work he began at Baptism:

> Yet furthermore man's mind is moved by the Holy Spirit, in order that he may attain the end of each work begun, and avoid whatever perils may threaten. This surpasses human nature: for sometimes it is not in a man's power to attain the end of his work, or to avoid evils or dangers, since these

may happen to overwhelm him in death. But the Holy Spirit works this in man, by bringing him to everlasting life, which is the end of all good deeds, and the release from all perils. *A certain confidence* of this is infused into the mind by the Holy Spirit Who expels any fear of the contrary. It is in this sense that fortitude is reckoned a gift of the Holy Spirit. For it has been stated above [I-II, q. 68, aa. 1, 2] that the gifts regard the motion of the mind by the Holy Spirit.[6]

St. Thomas realizes that none of us is strong or good enough to go even twenty-four hours without some rebellion of sin, some snarky word, or moment of jealous gossip. But if we allow the Holy Spirit to work his good deeds and release us from perils, a "certain confidence" (*quandam fiduciam*) or trust arises in the soul, assuring us that in our dwelling in the Spirit and his dwelling in us, a certain knowledge of our eternal bliss is granted to the soul, who keeps its eyes on God's power to save and not our own ability to sin.

So, we have seen how the Holy Spirit is the divine Person who unites us to the sacred humanity of Christ and thereby adopts us as children of the Father: "The Spirit itself bears witness with our spirit that we are chil-

---

[6] Thomas Aquinas, *Summa Theologiae* II-II, q. 139, a. 1; emphasis added.

dren of God, and if children, then heirs, heirs of God and joint heirs with Christ, if only we suffer with him so that we may also be glorified with him" (Rom 8:16–17). In making this room for the Divine Life in our souls, the Spirit also labors to remove any obstacles which might continue to keep God as second rate, preferring creatures over the Creator! This conviction of sin is just propae-deutic to an exponentially more important movement of the Spirit, with the purgation of our sin giving way to the illumination of our minds and then to the consecrated union which begins now and will continue in heavenly bliss forever.

CHAPTER 6

CHRIST FORMED DEEPLY WITHIN
(GAL 4:19)

Every Sunday and on major feasts, Catholics across the world profess the creed first written in 325, completed in 381, and tweaked a bit in the sixth century. It would be idolatry to place our Christian virtue of faith in anything other than God. We may *believe* another, but that is not the theological virtue at work; that is the goodness of human trust. But the theological virtues of faith, hope, and love are to find God and the affairs of God as their sole object.

So, while we may profess belief in "God the Father almighty," and in his "only Son our Lord," as well as "in the Holy Spirit, the Lord and the Giver of Life," how can we place our faith in "one, holy, Catholic, and apostolic Church"? Is this an obvious violation of the First Commandment and not having any other Gods than God alone that has escaped theological inquiry for seventeen hundred years? Hardly. The reason we are asked to place our faith in the Church is because, for Catholics at least, the Church is not a merely human enterprise. She is the Bride of Christ: divinely instituted, sustained, and destined.

That is why more traditional Catholics are careful to refer to the Church as "she" or "her," and not "it," trying to honor in speech and thought both the personal as well as the maternal and spousal nature of this gathering. This is because too many moderns think of the Church as just a religion or a set of beliefs or rules. While those codes are certainly present, the Church is not a "thing" or a building but a gathering of persons glued together by the love of the Holy Spirit and thus brought together before God as his spotless Bride. This chapter shall examine some ways we might think about this new way of being community, *ecclesia*—those called out of the world and into Christ.

Despite all the scandalous headlines of the past few decades, the Church somehow not only continues but is in fact flourishing in many places and ways. Not surprisingly, the recent outrages of sin and scandal are nothing new, a reminder that the Church does not gather saints but invites sinners in order to make them so. As Pope Francis is so fond of saying, the Church is not a museum for the righteous but more like a "field hospital" for the wounded and bloodied. This is not to make light of the lives ruined by some of the Church's ministers, but it is to point us to the fact that the Catholic Church is not nurtured by human virtue nor does it continue because of human wisdom or eloquence. Not long ago, one of my brightest students said she was finally ready to become Catholic, and in her excitement asked, "What should I do to prepare?" My answer? "Get ready to be disappointed."

Many centuries ago, Giovanni Boccaccio (d. 1375) put together one hundred short stories, many of which skewed organized religion and made fun of things many hold dear. In one of his tales, he recalls the story of a shrewd Jewish businessman from Paris named Abraham. After sensing something in his soul bidding him to join the Catholic Church, Abraham drew from his business savvy and decided he should first visit Rome to see for himself what kind of people this Roman Catholicism really produces. Afraid Abraham would witness the scurrilous clergy and gluttonous cardinals around the Roman Curia, Giannotto, one of Abraham's Catholic business partners, begged him to delay his trip to Rome and instead ask for Baptism first. Abraham remained resolute, visited Rome, and returned emphatic that he wanted to be Catholic now more than ever. Dumbfounded, Giannotto asked how this could be. "I see that what these scoundrel clerics so zealously want never takes root. But the exact opposite happens: despite them, your Church grows continually and shines more and more brightly." Therefore, Abraham concluded, "It is quite clear to me that your Church must have the Holy

Spirit for its foundation and support," arguing that the Church would have collapsed centuries ago were it not for her divine underpinnings and promises.[1]

Let us now look at three pieces of theology that help unfold this meaning of the Church as Christ's own Mystical Body. The first will be to look at the various ways this spiritual sense of the Church has been explained over the centuries. The second will concentrate on the first moment of incorporation into this Body, Christian Baptism, while the third section will focus on prayer and the Most Holy Eucharist, the "source and summit" of the Christian people.[2]

The Church as the Body of Christ

In fact, most of the Church Fathers described the Church as the very extension of Christ's own divine humanity, an embodied continuation which makes Christ available for those who lived after his bodily ascension into heaven:

> Christ and his Church thus together make up the "whole Christ," (*Christus totus*). The Church is

---

[1] Boccaccio, *Decameron* (New York: Penguin Books, 2003) 41, First Day, Second Story.

[2] Second Vatican Council, Constitution on the Church *Lumen Gentium* (November 21, 1964), §11; it is important to understand this phrase as orienting all Christians toward the Eucharist as the "source" that initiated the Church as well as the "summit" in that all Christian activity is directed toward perfect union with and through Christ in heaven.

one with Christ. The saints are acutely aware of this unity:

"Let us rejoice then and give thanks that we have become not only Christians, but Christ himself. Do you understand and grasp, brethren, God's grace toward us? Marvel and rejoice: we have become Christ. For if he is the head, we are the members; he and we together are the whole man. . . . The fullness of Christ then is the head and the members. But what does 'head and members' mean? Christ and the Church" (St. Augustine).

"Our redeemer has shown himself to be one person with the holy Church whom he has taken to himself" (Pope St. Gregory the Great).

"Head and members form as it were one and the same mystical person" (St. Thomas Aquinas, O.P.).

A reply of St. Joan of Arc to her judges sums up the faith of the holy doctors and the good sense of the believer: "About Jesus Christ and the Church, I simply know they're just one thing, and we shouldn't complicate the matter" (Acts of the Trial of Joan of Arc). (CCC §795)

This is the reality we have been exploring in these pages: love identifies itself with its beloved. God loved the world so much, he joined himself to our human nature and in so doing, formed a new people, a chosen race, a holy Church.

Throughout our Christian Tradition, it has really been the moment of Jesus's Transfiguration on Mount Tabor (Matt 17:1–8; Mark 9:2–8; Luke 9:28–36; see also 2 Pet 1:16–18) that most theologians have used to describe the first hint at how the divinity of Christ would shine through the rest of his Church. In the Mass's Preface for the Feast of the Transfiguration, the Church prays that the "scandal" the Pharisees and scribes sensed when imagining a vulnerable, fleshy God be removed from our minds so we are equipped to see how Jesus Christ, our Head, lived on earth and what our life, the life of his Body, might be as well:

V. The Lord be with you. R. And with your spirit.

V. Lift up your hearts. R. We lift them up to the Lord.

V. Let us give thanks to the Lord our God. R. It is right and just.

It is truly right and just, our duty and our salvation, always and everywhere to give you thanks, Lord, holy Father, almighty and eternal God, through Christ our Lord.

For he revealed his glory in the presence of chosen witnesses and filled with the greatest splendor that bodily form which he shares with all humanity, that the scandal of the Cross might be removed from the hearts of his disciples and that he might show how in the body of the whole Church is to be fulfilled what so wonderfully shone forth first in its Head.[3]

This scene captures precisely what the Incarnation is all about. Christ has taken on our dying human condition in order to unite it to Life himself and thus transform all that is human, all that could be moribund and decaying but need not be. In the glorious refulgence of his flesh appears the promise of Jesus's new life in each of us when we allow our humanity to be united to his.

This is why St. Paul likens Christian discipleship to this maturation of Christ's life in each of our souls: "My children, for whom I am again in labor until Christ be formed in you" (Gal 4:19). What it means to be deified is thus nothing more than Christ being formed within each of us, and this is the sole purpose of Christ founding a Church. Because the faithful have access to the Eucharistic Lord, we are able to imitate Mary and receive the Son of God's own Body and Blood into our very own bodies, into our own bloodstreams. This is the height of

---

[3] Preface for the Mass for the Feast of the Transfiguration.

love: the exchange and subsequent union of selves. Love is not mere affection or emotion; it is not simply wishing the other well. Love is ultimately marked by a mutual indwelling and identity, and Christ's Church was founded to be the locus of this tremendous drama of love.

Baptism

Baptism is the Christian answer to the Jewish rite of circumcision, that ritual which welcomes one into God's chosen people with a new indelible sign that this person has now been claimed for the Lord. But instead of being physical and limited to males only, Baptism is the initial manner by which God can allure all people into his kingdom. It was foreshadowed by God saving the Jewish people through the Red Sea, inaugurated by John the Baptist, and instituted by the Lord himself when he let St. John plunge him into the Jordan River. In so doing, Jesus gave us an example for how we imitate not only his life but also his death: "Or are you unaware that we who were baptized into Christ Jesus were baptized into his death?" (Rom 6:3). The threefold plunging into the holy water while calling upon the Father, the Son, and the Holy Spirit is a memorial of Christ's three days in the tomb, arising having conquered sin and death, a new life transmitted to us through the Rite of Baptism.

Treating this sacrament, the *Catechism* pulls together many of the themes we have already discussed in these pages:

Baptism not only purifies from all sins, but also makes the neophyte "a new creature," an adopted son [or daughter] of God, who has become a "partaker of the divine nature" (2 Pet 1:4), member of Christ and co-heir with him (1 Cor 6:15; 12:27; Rom 8:17), and a temple of the Holy Spirit (1 Cor 6:19). (CCC §1265)

And next,

The Most Holy Trinity gives the baptized sanctifying grace, the grace of justification: (1) enabling them to believe in God, to hope in him, and to love him through the theological virtues; (2) giving them the power to live and act under the prompting of the Holy Spirit through the gifts of the Holy Spirit; (3) allowing them to grow in goodness through the moral virtues. Thus the whole organism of the Christian's supernatural life has its roots in Baptism. (CCC §1266; format adjusted)

Appreciating what baptism has done for us usually involves the difficult fact that we do not remember being baptized; it is therefore incumbent upon the Christian faithful to try to understand the riches imparted to our souls at that moment. Here we were released from the ancient bond of sin incurred by Adam and Eve and made children of the New Adam and the New Eve, members of God's holy people, his Church.

In bringing us into the Mystical Body, baptism not only initiates our membership in God's Church, it enables us to call him Father. In fact, the Rite of Baptism ends with those present praying the one prayer Jesus himself taught us. But if we think about the "Our Father," we begin to realize that before Baptism neither of those words are true. I mean, how many of us use the royal "we"? As mere humans we say "I" or "my," but as valued members of Christ's Mystical Body, we now pray "Our." And "Father"? On the natural level, our fathers are mortal men named Jim and George, Joe and Geno. Yet in Baptism, we are adopted into a new relationship, calling God "Father," and by extension Mary our "Mother" and all the saints our eternal siblings. Would not the lives of Christians change if each actually believed this? As in any loving adoptive family, the adopted and the naturally-born children are not discriminated against. How much more does God the Father love his adopted children just as much as he loves his only-begotten Son? The genetic make-up and the manner by which each is a child of the Father may be different, but the love of the Father is the same: Jesus is Son by nature, we are sons and daughters through the grace of Baptism.

Baptism thus initiates our incorporation into the Body (*corpus*) of Christ. Accordingly, it is necessarily ordered to the neophyte's eventual reception of Holy Communion, the Body of Christ. Spiritual writers have stressed this convergence of terms and realities. So let us now see how the Most Holy Eucharist emerges in the Catholic Tradition as both the source of all grace as well as the pattern and model of what we, too, are meant to become.

Eucharist

Jesus himself promises us that if we allow his Body and Blood to enter our own bodies, we shall finally have true life within us: "Amen, amen, I say to you, unless you eat the flesh of the Son of Man and drink his blood, you do not have life within you. Whoever eats my flesh and drinks my blood has eternal life, and I will raise him on the last day. For my flesh is true food, and my blood is true drink. Whoever eats my flesh and drinks my blood remains in me and I in him" (John 6:53–56). It was well over a millennium until any Christian gave this and other related passages in Scripture a "symbolic" interpretation. The enfleshed God has promised us over and over that he "will not leave you orphans; I will come to you" (John 14:18) and that "I am with you always, until the end of the age" (Matt 28:20). So, how is the incarnate God present to us here and now? Do not let any Christian answer, "Well, he is with us spiritually." No, that is the prerogative of the Holy Spirit. The God-made-flesh is still with us in the Flesh and the Blood of the Sacrifice of the Mass, present in countless tabernacles across the globe, received every time we present ourselves for Holy Communion.

St. Augustine delivered a most beautiful homily forging a connection between this Body of Christ on the altar and the Body of Christ that we have become at baptism. This sermon was given on a Holy Saturday early in the fifth century in North Africa. It is important to know that in the early life of the Church, the non-baptized were welcome to come to Mass and to pray and to hear the Scriptures and, hopefully, a homily which might ignite a thirst for the truth of Christianity and admittance to Baptism. As such, Holy Saturday at the Easter Vigil was the first time new Christians were able to stay for the Creed, the Offertory, and for the Liturgy of the Eucharist. This is why Bishop Augustine orients these neophytes' eyes to the bread and wine they see for the first time on the altar. Augustine uses this opportunity to teach them that while their eyes see one thing—bread and wine—their faith tells them what these realities truly are, the Body and Blood of our Lord Jesus Christ. But then he quickly reminds them that they, too, have just become Christ's own Body and Blood:

> If you, therefore, are Christ's body and members, it is your own mystery that is placed on the Lord's table! It is your own mystery that you are receiving! You are saying "Amen" to what you are: your response is a personal signature, affirming your

faith. When you hear "The body of Christ," you reply "Amen." Be a member of Christ's body, then, so that your "Amen" may ring true! But what role does the bread play? We have no theory of our own to propose here; listen, instead, to what Paul says about this sacrament: "The bread is one, and we, though many, are one body" (see 1 Cor 10:17). Understand and rejoice: unity, truth, faithfulness, love. "One bread," he says. What is this one bread? Is it not the "one body," formed from many? Remember: bread doesn't come from a single grain, but from many. When you received exorcism, you were "ground." When you were baptized, you were "leavened." When you received the fire of the Holy Spirit, you were "baked." Be what you see; receive what you are.[4]

As in so many things, St. Augustine helped the Church formulate her teaching on what it means to be a Christian: it is not rule-following and pious recitation of prayers; it is literally to become Christ's Body, to become his living presence and power on earth.

As such, St. Augustine presents the Mass he celebrated daily in his cathedral in Hippo Regius not as a spectator sport during which the laity simply observe the

[4] Augustine, *Sermon* 272.

priest's movements. Rather, the Mass is the mystery of each of our lives—lives that are offered along with the bread and wine in order to be consecrated and brought into perfect communion with the Father. We are exorcised out of the fallen safety of our autonomy and first grafted onto a Church where we shall never again be alone. We are cleansed out of our fallen thirst not to matter and not to let anyone matter too deeply to us. We are then leavened with the holy waters of Baptism, made children of the Father as we emerge from the tomb with the Resurrected Christ. Finally, we are chrismated with the same oil the bishops use to ordain their priests—made one with the Anointed One whose sacrifice has redeemed the world.

In the center of the celebration of Holy Eucharist, there is a line in the rubrics instructing the priest to pray *secreto* in Latin or, as the Italians have rendered it, *sotto voce*, "in a hushed voice." Yet this line is so beautiful and it captures the heart of the Christian mystery so well, I find myself praying it more *voce* than *sotto*: "By the mystery of this water and wine, may we come to share in the divinity of Christ who humbled himself to share in our humanity." That is, as the priest dribbles just a drop of water into a chalice of wine, he prays that as these two elements become one, we mortals may come to partake of Christ's Divine Nature, now made accessible to us through his humble humanity.

Charles Williams (d. 1945) was one of the Oxford Inklings, a group of friends who gathered periodically to discuss their literary interests, including C. S. Lewis, J. R. R. Tolkien, and others. One day, the friends challenged whether Charles loved them, and he so simply but so sagaciously retorted, "Love you? I am you."[5] Even a glimpse of this answer should cause our hearts to leap. The real lover's weal and woe is found not in himself or herself but in the heart of his or her beloved. This is the entire purpose of the Incarnation, and our personal prayer life should always keep this in mind. Instead of simply reciting prayers, however beautiful, we should do so with this always in our consciousness: *I read the words of Jesus. I behold him in the Sacred Host. I see his life's mysteries through the eyes of Our Lady in the Rosary. All of this and more because I want to become like the One who has so lovingly and freely identified himself with me.*

This is the grace we should seek whenever we go to Eucharistic Adoration. Recall John the Evangelist's claim in 1 John 3:2 that we shall *become like God by seeing him.* This is not some heavenly abstraction but a recognition that we become like those people with whom we spend the most time. We long to become like those whom we love the most. We see this phenomenon all the time: the

---

[5] As recalled in C. S. Lewis, *The Four Loves* (New York: HarperOne [1960] 2017), 122.

elderly couple who have shared a lifelong love of the same pastimes, programs, foods, and family together. We see this in the first blush of love when a young man sees in this beautiful woman the tenderness and compassion, the wit and the wisdom he desires for himself as well as for the family which he has always wanted. We see it even in sub-human relationships: the enthusiast who "becomes" like that which takes his time—whether it be one's passions of fishing or golf or even a beloved pet.

Prayer

In the monstrance, we see a God who has lowered himself into what appears as bread, calibrating his greatness to our littleness, doing whatever he can so that we might allow him into ourselves. As we gaze upon that miraculous Host of pure white, let us be absorbed into that face so as to let it be conformed to our own countenance ever more each day. The celebration of the Holy Mass, the recitation of the Divine Office, the praying of the Rosary, and so many other centuries-old devotions are beautiful and necessary tools with which to grow in godly union. But there is no substitute for the surrender of our most inner selves with our own personal words and histories to the One who awaits such bare transparency from those who can be so easily content with the superficial.

That is why we must pray from our own words, out of our own experience. Before the Host, during those prayerful pauses during the Mass, or anywhere we can settle ourselves, we must look for ways to pour out our heart's desires and finally be rid of any melancholy or self-doubt which keeps us owning our own belovedness before the Father. Let us talk to the Lord as a friend, another self, for he has stripped himself of all power and pretense so we who are ultimately powerless and yet proud, can come to him without fear of being turned away. If we do not make time to be with quiet and still with the Lord in our own life's stories, the world will drag us into its story. We teeter between the values of this world and of Christ's Body; we are so often torn between the sad ennui of this world burdened by strife while also being invited to the intimacy and peace Jesus alone can offer:

> You withdraw into your sorrow: this, at least, is yours. In the experience of your woes you feel yourself alive. . . . But since you are so wounded, and the open torment of your heart has opened up the abyss of your very self, put out your hand to me and, with it, feel the pulse of another Heart: through this new experience your soul will surrender and heave up the dark gall which it has long collected. I must overpower you. I cannot spare exacting from you your melancholy—your most-loved possession. Give it to me, even if . . . your inner-self thinks it must die. Give me this idol,

this cold stony clot in your breast and in its place I will give you a new heart of flesh that will beat to the pulse of my own Heart. Give me this self of yours, which lives on its not being able to live, which is sick because it cannot die. Let it perish, and you will finally begin to live. . . . Dare to leap into the light! Do not take the world to be more profound than God! . . . What could be simpler and sweeter than opening the door of love? What could be easier than falling to one's knees and saying, "My Lord and my God?"[6]

Like St. Thomas who rejoiced when he saw the Lord's own pierced side and hands, we can finally enter a wound that heals, a Blood that quenches, a Body that embraces without qualification or objectification. We can finally cry out with the one who so famously doubted, "My Lord and my God" (John 20:28).

When we are finally feeling filled, those growing in holiness often next find themselves thirsting to intercede for both loved ones as well as the world in general. A theology of the Mystical Body understands this desire for intercessory petition, knowing that when we lift our broken world up to the Father, joined by our prayers to the Son's own pierced hands, we can actually find a joy

---

6 Hans Urs von Balthasar, *Heart of the World*, trans. Erasmo Leiva (San Francisco: Ignatius Press, [1954] 1997), 164–65.

that helps heal the Body of Christ on earth. "Now I rejoice in my sufferings for your sake, and in my flesh I am filling up what is lacking in the afflictions of Christ on behalf of his body, which is the Church" (Col 1:24). The ascended Body of Christ, now seated at the Father's right hand, suffers no more; the Eucharistic Body can sustain no injury. But the Mystical Body still groans for completion, and when serious Christians unite their sufferings to her groans, God's grace is once again brought to earth through the free assent of a creature. The soul who is even partially aware of how Christ longs to extend his life into her realizes the power of not living and acting alone. This is why the Apostle Paul instructs to "pray without ceasing" (1 Thess 5:17), knowing how the deified soul enjoys divine warmth at every moment of her existence and how "through desire and affection and the union of love [Jesus] makes of her another himself."[7]

7 Catherine of Siena, the "Prologue" to her famous treatise, *The Dialogue*; slightly adjusted. *Catherine of Siena: The Dialogue*, trans. Suzanne Noffke, O.P. (New York: Paulist Press, 1980), 25.

·⟨≋⟩·

CHAPTER 7

LISTENING TO LEWIS, HEARING A
"LITTLE CHRIST"(LUKE 10:16)

The first text I have my first-year students read in Theology 1000 is C. S. Lewis's classic *Mere Christianity*. They know this English author mainly through his *Chronicles of Narnia*, and most of my students are intrigued to find out what a serious Christian Lewis came to be later in life. Since this text is such a classic and since it is central to Christian apologists, both Catholic and Protestant, let us use this chapter to explore what Lewis advances in this book: his notion of becoming *little Christs*. Lewis admits that *Mere Christianity* is not a confessional work but is "merely" the explanation and defense of "the belief that has been common to nearly all Christians at all times" (Introduction).[1] *Mere Christianity* continues to prove

---

[1] Since there is no uniform pagination for all the various editions of *Mere Christianity*, I shall simply include the Book and Section number parenthetically after each quote. An earlier version of this essay appeared as "Mere Christianity: Theosis in a British Way," *The Journal*

to be a seminal work of Christian educators teaching at most levels of formation, so it is especially important to understand what this one "belief . . . common to nearly all Christians" may be. What Lewis then describes as "putting on Christ" or "dressing up" as a child of the Father "is not one among many jobs a Christian has to do; and it is not a sort of special exercise for the top class. It is the whole of Christianity. Christianity offers nothing else at all" (IV.8).

A Brief Biography and Summary

When Jesus promises his followers that, "Whoever listens to you listens to me" (Luke 10:16), we should become more insistent on prayer and study, ensuring that our thoughts and words reflect the Lord's as closely as possible. The Catholic Church has an official community of those who have echoed the Lord's life most faithfully and vibrantly—the saints—but Lewis is one of those voices outside the Church's canonized sons and daughters who speaks for Christ in an unmatchable way. Clive Staples Lewis was born in Northern Ireland in 1898, and having seen the worst of both Catholic and Protestant in his boyhood home of Belfast, he grew up very suspicious of the central claims of a faith that preached peace and fraternal charity. Through his later study and community of friends—mainly through reading the works of the Scottish minister George MacDonald (1824–1905) and his many illuminating conversations with his Catholic colleague J. R. R. Tolkien (1892–1973)—Lewis returned to the Christianity of his youth, but now with sincerity and a desire to make the name of Christ resound in every generation. Lewis never became Catholic, but he has certainly helped open that door for many to be received today.

What became this classic work, *Mere Christianity*, actually began as BBC radio talks during the war-torn years of 1941–44. This was a time of strong English Catholicism, readers devouring all they could from G. K. Chesterton, Ronald Knox, Hillaire Belloc, Frank Sheed, and Maisie Ward, as well as spiritual writers like Evelyn Underhill and Caryll Houselander. In fact, throughout her 1941 work, *This War is the Passion* (one can hear a theology of deification even in the title, seeing how the cross is being played out still today in the fight between good and evil), Houselander popularized the term "little Christ." We do not know whether Lewis had read any Houselander before he went on the air in 1941, but it is clear that such mystical incorporation of the Christian into Christ was very much the theological tenor of those war years.

Book I: Under a Law Not Made by Creatures
Book I of *Mere Christianity*, "Right and Wrong as a Clue to the Meaning of the Universe," introduces this ultimate

Meaning by way of the human mind. Lewis opens *Mere Christianity* by highlighting the created soul as the locus where one will discover God. There is a drama occurring within each human person who naturally discerns "right" from "wrong," "is" from "ought," which leads each of us to the very nature of the divine. That is, in the human person's need to make sense of the changing world around them, we come to recognize the presence of One higher than we, One who is necessarily distinct from our own civil conventions and accrued social habits. Unlike other visible creatures, we may become satisfied with what "is," but deep down we often know that we "ought" to be acting and thinking otherwise. As such, Lewis makes us all face a hard fact: we all love what is right when it is advantageous towards us, and we struggle to embrace what is true when it disadvantages or asks us to go without.

Yet this struggle shows that all humans have an inclination toward absolute truth, that we all are oriented toward doing what is right. This then leads us to a more accurate and thorough understanding of the nature of the God who created us: "That the Being behind the universe is intensely interested in right conduct—in fair play, unselfishness, courage, good faith, honesty and truthfulness" (I.5). Lewis thus demands that the presence behind the Moral Law is not simply some universal (although it is that), but also a Person who can relate to face-to-face with those under the Moral Law. That is precisely why we come to know God by examining other persons: "You find out more about God from the Moral Law than from the universe in general just as you find out more about a man by listening to his conversation than by looking at a house he has built" (I.5). Lewis's explication of the Moral Law is thus God's conversation with those made in his image and likeness. While other divine traces (vestigial) in creation may point to some divine attributes, the human person is uniquely poised to reveal more about God than any other creature; made in the divine image, the *imago Dei* possesses an innate relationality to the divine.

Book II: Knowing God by Knowing Truth

In Book II, "What Christians Believe," Lewis accordingly focuses the reader's attention on how this divine Being discerned throughout Book I is neither some capricious force nor some impish scamp. Rather, this is a God who is pure reason, who resonates perfectly and personally with goodness, and who tolerates evil only in order to bring all rebellion freely back to faithfulness in him. Lewis's emphasis on the role of free will within the drama of salvation here is splendid and is reminiscent of the Church Fathers who also understood sin as the perverse imitation of godliness. That is, Lewis understands the entire Gospel message is one of transformative love, but love must be freely chosen and appropriated: "Free will, though it makes evil possible, is also the only thing that makes possible any love or goodness or joy worth having. . . . The happiness which God designs for His higher creatures is the happiness of being freely, voluntarily united to Him and to each other in an ecstasy of love." (II.3). If God is going to relate to us as other persons and not as mere automata, he must allow us to turn away from him.

But Lewis also knows that even in our turning away, we are showing our innate desire to be like God. He therefore explains sin as perverse imitation of the very God whom we are created to be like. In other words, the Enemy knew that no other temptation could have moved the first couple out of Eden, out of the "natural" perfection they enjoyed. This explains why Lewis presents his understanding of sin in terms of our innate yearning for divinity. The "Dark Power" promises our protoparents that they could be "like gods" (Gen 3:5). In one way, this was true, and that is why Lewis refuses to name this an act of mendacity. He instead argues that human sinfulness comes not from believing a lie but from a seeking divinity apart from the divine. What else could the Enemy of our human nature have used to tempt us?

As we have seen, on the natural level, Adam and Eve had everything; if anything, this is precisely what Eden is to represent. The only blessing the first couple lacked was that full and deified union with God, which was the one and only thing which Satan could have used to tempt them. No other good could have been a temptation, for every other good they possessed perfectly and in abundance. Lewis realizes that, while we are created so as to become godly, this can occur only in union with the Triune God in whose image and likeness each human person has been made. Satan did not so much lie as he usurped a power and a privilege which was never his to bestow. Lewis hence likens human excellence to an automobile which can run on only the proper petroleum. Like an automobile, God alone can be the petrol which produces the types of human persons he intended: "God cannot give us a happiness and peace apart from Himself, because it is not there. There is no such thing" (II. 3).

Here Lewis moves from the internal transformation necessary to live the Christ-life to the ethical demands made by such rebirth. The law no longer saves, but only Christ's dwelling within the human soul brings true life. This new self in Christ is, therefore, no longer an autonomous "I," but it becomes a mystical "we," as the indwelling Christ now activates how the Christian thinks and speaks and acts. By stressing this new sense of union between God and creature, I am better able to show why Book III, "Christian Behaviour," argues that true moral excellence is not a matter of becoming a Victorian dandy, pristinely polished and all cleaned up, but more a matter of being transformed into a new type of human:

> There are lots of things which your conscience
> might not call definitely wrong (specially things
> in your mind) but which you will see at once you
> cannot go on doing if you are seriously trying to
> be like Christ. For you are no longer thinking
> simply about right and wrong; you are trying to
> catch the good infection from a Person. It is more
> like painting a portrait than like obeying a set of
> rules. . . . The real Son of God is at your side. He
> is beginning to turn you into the same kind of
> thing as Himself. He is beginning, so to speak, to
> "inject" His kind of life and thought, His *Zoe*, into
> you; beginning to turn the tin soldier into a live
> man. (IV.7)

Lewis's understanding of morality makes no sense without this Christ-likeness as the goal of all action. This is
why Book III is devoid of any practical ethical quanda-
ries or concrete steps of practical action; the purpose of
Christian morality is not *doing* any particular right action,
but it is *becoming* the type of person each of us has been
created to be.

Book III: Becoming What You Do

Lewis thus understands that for the Christian, the moral
life is the joyful life. For those living their lives in Christ,

there is no dissonance between desires and actions. Christian morality is not a matter of fulfilling one's duty, nor is it simply a matter of doing the right thing. It is a matter of right relationship: of becoming the kind of creature (personal morality) who does well to and alongside others (social ethics) who are all called to be united by the same goal and God (the ultimate purpose of all human activity), Lewis's three areas of Christian behavior. As such, Book III surveys the factors central to any introduction to the moral life in terms of relation: the properly-aligned soul enjoying mastery over the lower passions and carnal desires, the beautiful relationship between men and women, and ultimately the relationship between God and humanity.

Whereas Lewis's soteriology throughout *Mere Christianity* is markedly Augustinian in its emphasis on properly-ordered loves and the drama of conversion, Lewis's moral theology is decidedly Thomistic. Lewis understands that the virtues he traces in Book III do not give their possessors true life but are instead there "to prevent a breakdown, or a strain, or a friction, in the running of that machine," the human soul (III.1). As St. Thomas Aquinas himself notes, the moral virtues do not advance a soul's salvation. The moral virtues are operative and efficient only when informed by charity. In Christian ethics, love of God and love of neighbor is the only "the bond of perfection" (Col 3:14) because what sanctifies and saves is not some internal amelioration but the love of God and love of neighbor. Alone, temperance, fortitude, prudence, and justice do not better the soul; they simply keep the soul from getting worse. The human person's true growth must be effected through love, as the one reality which alone can mend and transform men and women forever.

When reading *Mere Christianity* in light of the overall aim of this book in explaining a theology of human deification, it is the virtue of hope that stands out most audaciously. As we come to learn throughout Book III, Christianity is not ultimately about doing right or avoiding wrong. In this sense Christianity is not a religion at all; it is a relationship that demands our free assent and subsequent vulnerability as we allow Christ to lead us into his very self. It is no longer about keeping the law or about carefully fixing our eyes on our own successes or failings, but about casting our very beings upon the Lord himself. That is why throughout Book III of *Mere Christianity*, Lewis is intent upon avoiding two errors: (1) Morality is not God's maneuver to spoil people's fun, (2) nor is the Christian ethical code meant simply to make one stronger or more efficient in his or her tasks. This is why Lewis can later so beautifully teach that, "God became man to turn creatures into [children]: not simply to produce better men of the old kind but to produce a new kind of man.

It is not like teaching a horse to jump better and better but like turning a horse into a winged creature" (IV. 10). Deification does not abolish humanity's nature but fulfills and completes it.

Book IV: Becoming "Little Christs"

Book IV, "Beyond Personality: Or First Steps in the Doctrine of the Trinity," is where Lewis's appreciation for human divinization reaches its crescendo. Book IV accordingly begins by reaffirming that, at its core, Christianity is neither a moral code nor simply another religion (see IV.1). As important as dogma and doctrine and a code of ethics may be for any creed, Christianity is not so much a religion as it is a relationship. It is ultimately a matter of Lewis's exhortation throughout Book IV that we become "little Christs." But if this is true, what good is dogma, and what does solid doctrinal theology matter?

One of Lewis's great gifts to the post-Enlightenment world was to show that dogma does matter, that what one holds to be true (if anything) cannot but shape how they live (if at all). Think of the Father of the Enlightenment, Immanuel Kant's (d. 1804) notorious rejection of this connection between beliefs and behavior: "Whether we are to worship three or ten persons in the Deity makes no difference."[2] But it does, of course, matter. As we saw

---

[2] Immanuel Kant, *Der Streit der Fakultäten* (Germany: Volker Gerhardt, 1798), 7.39.

back in chapter 4, it very much matters that Christians from Nicaea onward are to place their gift of faith in "one Lord Jesus Christ, the Only Begotten Son of God, born of the Father before all ages. God from God, Light from Light, true God from true God, begotten, not made, consubstantial with the Father." *Begotten, not made.* This is a doctrine with the most important implication ever: there are two ways of being a child of the Father: (1) as the Only Son who is so because he is begotten naturally before all ages and so consubstantial with the Father, and (2) as those sons and daughter who have been supernaturally adopted, and although their substance is forever created and human, have been made co-heirs with Christ to enjoy the same filiality before the Father.

This is why Lewis next writes how the one Son, "came to this world and became a man in order to spread to other men the kind of life He has—by what I call "good infection." Every Christian is to become a little Christ. The whole purpose of becoming a Christian is simply nothing else" (IV.4). When this happens, we are no longer confined to our merely created humanity, what Lewis rightly calls in section 5 "*Bios* or natural life," but we can, instead, live at a new level of reality in Christ, "the *Zoe*, the uncreated life" (IV.5). By contrasting these two Greek words for "life," Lewis wants to teach us that in Christ, one moves from merely living (*bios*) to truly flourishing (*zoe*), from existing to excellence.

Deification is what the Catholic Intellectual Tradition calls this true life in Christ, the result of those who are created in Christ's image and likeness, allowing Christ to enter their souls freely and without reserve. Only then are supernatural powers planted within the human soul thus enabling it to do superhuman things, like believe, hope, and love. Christ in the soul transforms the soul into his own self, his viceroy, as the vine sends its own life through the branches. Jesus's humble desire for all men and women is to make each his own, to transform us into "mirrors" and "carriers" of his own Divine Life: "turning you permanently into a different sort of thing; into a new little Christ, a being which, in its own small way, has the same kind of life as God; which shares in His power, joy, knowledge and eternity" (IV.7).

The phrase most readily associated with C. S. Lewis was coined by a Puritan divine almost a half-millennium ago. Richard Baxter (1615–91) saw in "mere Christianity" the fundamental beliefs that both unite all disciples of Christ as well as separate Christians from all others. What no seventeenth-century Puritan Christianity was able to admit, however, was the "merest" of all Christian convictions: that God became human so humans could become one with God. It took the splintering of the twentieth century for Christianity to recover this ancient doctrine, and for many, it took the blessed genius of Lewis to make it so intelligible.

C. S. Lewis's *Mere Christianity* is a multi-faceted work of theology and an unmatchable piece of contemporary apologetics. Through all its many wonderful side streets and turns is one underlying thesis: God created other persons so they would freely choose to become like him and so live with him in perfect intimacy forever. And when the beauty of creation, the morality of conscience, and the keeping of the law all failed, God sent his only Son into human flesh. This Son lived the human life fully for no other reason than to continue his own Divine Life into each and every human soul. He became the Son of man so we could all become the sons and daughters of God. In this "great exchange," God thus not only becomes one of us, each of us is called to become God, to becoming living members of his own Body as the Christ-life is extended through us into every time and place. This is both the mere-ness and the majesty of all life in Christ.

CHAPTER 8

SEEING, SERVING CHRIST IN OTHERS
(MATT 25:40)

There is an unfortunate divide between many in Christ's Church who pray so beautifully at Eucharistic Adoration and those who serve the homeless and the poor so faithfully throughout the week through various organizations. There is overlap and certainly much more than in ages past. Yet we still tend to think of deep intimate prayer and performing the almsdeeds as two separate activities that speak to two different sorts of people. This is not what Jesus intended nor what he wants for us going forward. Those who understand Christ's divine presence in the Holy Eucharist must also be the ones who seek ways to attend to their brothers, sisters, and neighbors; those who are instinctively activist and socially-minded must also make time for silent Adoration in order to prioritize their souls rightly and serve others charitably.

This chapter wants to make this connection between

Catholic social thought and our insistence that the goal of the Christian life is to become another Christ. The Church Fathers were keenly aware of this union, which in our efficiently driven world (and oftentimes, Church), we forget and concentrate only on the "doing good," as it drifts further and further from a life of prayer and intercession. But, in the teaching of St. Augustine of Hippo, "We must understand this person as ourselves, as the person of our Church, the one person that is Christ's body.... The sufferings of Christ are therefore not undergone by Christ alone; yet in another sense, we can say that the sufferings of Christ are endured nowhere else but in Christ."[1] Let us now explore this unity running throughout the Church's seamless theology between the active and the contemplative life, beginning with a startling recovery of the threefold Body of Christ.

Jesus's Threefold Body

We have been stressing a Christian doctrine that when verbalized in this way, may seem quite shocking, but the

---

[1] Augustine, *Commentary on the Psalms* 61.4. St. Augustine is a master of exhorting his parishioners to live out a theology of the Mystical Body: e.g., "Now, however, I wonder if we shouldn't have a look at ourselves, if we shouldn't think about his body, because he is also us. After all, if we weren't him, this wouldn't be true: *When you did it for one of the least of mine, you did it for me* (Matt 25:40). If we weren't him, this wouldn't be true: *Saul, Saul, why are you persecuting me?* (Acts 9:4). So we too are him, because we are his organs, because we are his body, because he is our head, because the whole Christ is both head and body" (*Sermon* 133.8).

Body of Jesus Christ can be said to be encountered in three different ways. For Christ himself teaches us that his very body born of a Virgin is also encountered in the Eucharist he instituted for all time on Holy Thursday, which, in turn, is to be fed and clothed and visited in his Mystical Body: "Whatever you did for one of these least brothers or sisters of mine, you did for me" (Matt 25:40). Such an expansive awareness of the Incarnation began in St. Ambrose (d. 397), the great bishop of schism-torn Milan in the fourth century, and most certainly the one who introduced this line of thinking into his most famous convert, St. Augustine of Hippo. Commenting on the Scriptures, Bishop Ambrose preached to the Catholics in the Milanese Cathedral: "We have no doubt as to what is meant by body, especially if we remember that Joseph of Arimathea received the Body from Pilate. . . . But the Body is also the subject of his saying: my flesh is real food indeed . . . and this Body is also that of the Church."[2]

Once the Church was settled into centuries of Eucharistic reflection and medieval universities and monasteries of study were flourishing, this insight became standard, and a technical vocabulary arose (as it did for most things with the sophisticated medieval mind)—namely, that the physical body born of the Virgin (*corpus natum*) gives way on Holy Thursday Eve to the Eucharistic Body (*corpus*

---

[2] Ambrose of Milan, *Homily on Luke* 17.37.

eucharisticum) but then beautifully and perhaps most mysteriously into the Mystical Body (*corpus mysticum*), the Church, your neighbor. This is what these university doctors and scholarly saints called the *triplex modus corporis*—the three-fold manner of Christ's Body and his way of being present in this world.[3]

While this may sound dogmatically abstract, think of how any person comes into the world in the best of all circumstances. The first place a child is entrusted to is (what should be) the safest place on earth, in the womb of his or her mother. After nine months of nourishing intimacy, that child is next delivered to a family structure where, hopefully, dad and perhaps brothers and sisters begin to interact with him or her as well. Here trust begins as this person is now knowing and is being known by others who have been close for some time. From there eventually comes the introduction to a much wider community: meeting a wider circle of family, playmates, the first day of school, and so on. This third entrustment is the wildest and least controllable, but with anticipation over the years of familial trust and reliable friendships, this little person is ready to meet the world.

This is how the Body of Christ came into the world as well. The Son of God first emptied himself (Phil 2:7) into

---

[3] For the history of this "threefold Body," see Jean Borella, *The Sense of the Supernatural* (Edinburgh: T & T Clark, 1998), 69–77.

the virginal womb of Mother Mary. Here for many months, the secret remained just between baby and mother—a new life ushered in, a small tiny presence of the eternal on earth. Here was God's Body, words next spoken the night before he died. Here Jesus next entrusted himself into the hands of his first priests, the Apostles in the Upper Room: "[T]his is my body" (Matt 26:26, Mark 14:22; Luke 22:19). But the messiest handing over was yet to come: as our Savior was crucified on the Cross, when he descended into the hell of the human condition and then rose anew, he thereby placed himself in the hearts of all men and women. This drawn-out formation of his Mystical Body was thus quiet and relatively safe, beginning with the gentle care of Mary, but then became riskier when he delivered himself into the hands of holy but sinful men, his first priests at the Last Supper, and then came the most radical entrustment of all, identifying himself with all humanity, especially "the least" of his sisters and brothers whom he has now mystically become.

As this ancient theology was being normalized and made part of the Church's Tradition, bishops and monastic leaders were preaching how their congregations and religious brothers and sisters had to work to unite their labors within the Church walls and the injustices they encountered out on the world's streets. Behind these various exhortations, we see how this connection between Christ, the Most Blessed Sacrament, and our neighbor has been part of the Church's teaching forever. Think, for example, of how St. Basil the Great (d. 379) could ask his congregations throughout Asia Minor to reflect on all the Lord's blessings to them and to sift through their closets and pantries to imitate God and give to others as he has given to them:

> Now, someone who takes a man who is clothed and renders him naked would be termed a robber; but when someone fails to clothe the naked, while he is able to do this, is such a man deserving of any other appellation? The bread which you hold back belongs to the hungry; the coat, which you guard in your locked storage-chests, belongs to the naked; the footwear mouldering in your closet belongs to those without shoes. The silver that you keep hidden in a safe place belongs to the one in need. Thus, however many are those whom you could have provided for, so many are those whom you wrong.[4]

Or another great bishop active in the fourth century, St. John Chrysostom, the Bishop of Constantinople (d. 407), could instruct his priests and his people in no uncertain terms that:

> Do you want to honor Christ's body? Then do not

---

[4] Basil the Great, *Homily on the Saying of the Gospel According to Luke*, "I will pull down my barns and build bigger ones," §7.

scorn him in his nakedness, nor honor him here in the Church with silken garments while neglecting him outside where he is cold and naked. For he who said: *This is my body*, and made it so by his words, also said: *You saw me hungry and did not feed me, and inasmuch as you did not do it for one of these, the least of my brothers, you did not do it for me.* What we do here in the church requires a pure heart, not special garments; what we do outside requires great dedication. . . .

For God does not want golden vessels but golden hearts. . . . Of what use is it to weigh down Christ's table with golden cups, when he himself is dying of hunger? First, fill him when he is hungry; then use the means you have left to adorn his table. Will you have a golden cup made but not give a cup of water? What is the use of providing the table with cloths woven of gold thread, and not providing Christ himself with the clothes he needs? What profit is there in that? Tell me: If you were to see him lacking the necessary food but were to leave him in that state and merely surround his table with gold, would he be grateful to you or rather would he not be angry? . . . Do not, therefore, adorn the church and ignore your afflicted brother, for he is the most precious temple of all.[5]

The Church's gold and linen and even the Most Holy Eucharist will no longer be present in heaven, when the Lord Jesus is finally encountered without any veiling of his Flesh and Blood. The one constant from this world to the next, then, are our brothers and sisters whom we must even now pray to see as other Christs, other Marys.

We have been emphasizing the fact that what makes all Christians is the fact that the Son of God became human. No other religion believes that God came to earth to save us; no other creed believes that God saves us as one of us. As a result, every Christian must believe that in the womb of the Blessed Virgin Mary, God united to himself our very own mortal body and blood and all that makes us human. Here, God takes on a physical, historically real body. Continuing, as we saw above, the night before this God-made-man died and knowing he would thereafter ascend to the Father, he took a piece of unleavened bread and declared, "Now, this is my body." Here through the Eucharistic Body, the incarnate God-man keeps his promise of never abandoning us, of being with us until the end of the world, and so on.

But call to mind something you have seen most of your life: that Eucharistic Body does not have ears to lis-

<hr/>

[5]   John Chrysostom, *Homily on Matthew* 50:3–4.

ten to the lonely, does not have feet to visit the shut-in, does not have a mouth to counsel the seeking nor hands to help those in need. But you and I do. We are the Mystical Body. This is where the incarnate Son of God also dwells. This is how Jesus can assure us that, "Whatever you did for one of the least of these brothers and sisters of mine, you did for me" (Matt 25:40 NIV). It is how Saul can hear from the heavens as he is rampantly persecuting the first generation of Christian disciples, "Saul, Saul, why are you persecuting me?" (Acts 9:4). The marginalized Christ calls his own; his faithful, Christ identifies with himself. This is the ultimate effect of charity—uniting Lover and beloved, making one flesh.

The Church's theology of deification insists on the unity and inseparability of this triplex Body. Every Christian has to assent to the biological body of Christ now seated at the right hand of the Father. Catholics are blessed to have held tightly to the centrality of this Body now being performed in a sacramental manner, making the Incarnation not just a distant memory or a future encounter, but that Jesus Christ—God made flesh—is still Emmanuel, God with us. But we will all become saints only if we allow this same Jesus to meet us in his Mystical Body, in his rag-tag beggars at the exit ramps of our pedestrian-less cities, in the people we find naturally unlikeable, in the day-to-day encounters of all those Christ puts into our lives.

For too long, the Church's social thought and devotional practices have been divided and thus isolated in the souls of many of her children. Sadly, on a university campus, for instance, there are often the students who are eager to serve the homeless and the poor around our urban area, and then there are those who are the first to sign up for Eucharistic Adoration and lead the Rosary. While both of these sets of activities are meritorious and necessary in their own right, the Church's theology of deification insists that the two inform and feed off one another. That is, without deep transformative prayer, the almsdeeds remain only good works—helpful for the needy but falling short of the charity and dignity Christ wills we impart to one another; conversely, without an attention to the needs of others, prayer and devotions without action remain sterile and fall short of Jesus's command to love him in the least of his brothers and sisters. How often has each of us looked away from someone begging for money, begging for our attention? How many times have I pulled into the far exit lane so as to avoid eye contact with that person who is always standing there with his empty hand out? What is even worse, I sometimes grab my rosary beads as a way of looking engaged and serious and just so happened not to have seen that lowdown. How this must sadden our Lord who, in no uncertain terms, tells us that whatever we do to the least of our brothers and sisters, we do to him.

Catholic social teaching is characterized by this connection between the ongoing Incarnation and the Church's insistence on justice for all. This tradition has fought a long ideological battle with other ways of approaching one's neighbor, especially those political and economic systems which tend to reduce the individual to a faceless number:

> The Church has rejected the totalitarian and atheistic ideologies associated in modern times with "communism" or "socialism." She has likewise refused to accept, in the practice of "capitalism," individualism and the absolute primacy of the law of the marketplace over human labor. Regulating the economy solely by centralized planning perverts the basis of social bonds; regulating it solely by the law of the marketplace fails social justice, for "there are many human needs which cannot be satisfied by the market." Reasonable regulation of the marketplace and economic initiatives, in keeping with a just hierarchy of values and a view to the common good, is to be commended. (CCC §2425)

If we humans were the highest beings, perhaps politics

and economics would be the worthiest pursuits. But as we all deeply realize at some tender point in our lives, we are made for much more than just worldly honor or sensual comforts, as welcome as those can be.

The Church's social agenda is and always has been rooted in prayer and proper worship. No mere human can love and serve faithfully in the manner a person deserves, but Christ can. This is why we must receive him first in order to attend to others properly. Whereas an unbridled capitalism can objectify others and see them only as economic opportunities, and whereas socialism and communism treat everyone and everything as a product of the state (including the family as well as human life), Catholicism sees each and every human person as an eternal gift, divinely desired and worthy of all our care, both bodily as well as spiritual.

The Church's social message is thus one of both worldly cunning—astutely addressing structures of exploitation in their many forms—while subordinating any strategy needed to combat injustices to the eternal worth and dignity all deserve who are made in God's own image and likeness. Or as C. S. Lewis put it, "Next to the Blessed Sacrament itself, your neighbor is the holiest object presented to your senses. If he is your Christian neighbor, he is holy in almost the same way, for in him also Christ *vere latitat*—the glorifier and the glorified, Glory himself is truly hidden.[6]

The Deifying Disguise:
Loving Christ in Loving Neighbor

If anyone of recent memory lived out this connection, it would be Mother Teresa, St. Teresa of Calcutta (d. 1997). Most of us know her story, feeling a "call within a call" to serve the lowliest of the low, thus finding herself in the poorest slums of the most impoverished cities of India. From morning to night, she poured herself out so others could not only eat and be bathed, but so that they might know their human dignity as well as their belovedness before the Father. As draining as this life of service left her, she never wavered in keeping God and neighbor in union. In Mother Teresa we find a woman who adored our God in heaven with an intensity that often left her desiccated and confused about how close God really was in her, a woman who spent hours before the Blessed Sacrament and received our Eucharistic Lord daily for decades, and a woman who spent her life serving the poorest of the poor.

It is no wonder, then, that one of the Church's new-

---

[6] This comes from the very last line of C. S. Lewis's famous homily entitled "Weight of Glory," from *The Weight of Glory and Other Addresses* (New York: HarperCollins, 2001), 46, which Lewis delivered at Oxford University's Church of St. Mary the Virgin, on June 8, 1941; the Latin he uses here, *vere latitat*, could be translated, "truly, he [God] hides."

est saints can provide the modern world with the insight that how we pray and how we serve must converge in the Christ, united to his Cross and Resurrection:

> Our life is linked to the Eucharist. Through faith in and love of the body of Christ under the appearance of bread, we take Christ literally: "I was hungry and you gave me food. I was a stranger and you welcomed me, naked and you clothed me." The Eucharist is connected with the passion. I was giving Communion this morning—my two fingers were holding Jesus. Try to realize that Jesus allows Himself to be broken. The Eucharist involves more than just receiving; it also involves satisfying the hunger of Christ. He says, "Come to me." He is hungry for souls.[7]

Recognizing Christ's hunger for souls meant that the saint of Calcutta also had to recognize that soul's hunger—a hunger for food which was only surpassed by a hunger for love. That is how she was able to hold in harmonic unison the body of the historical Christ, the Body of the Eucharistic Lord, and the body of the leper dying in Calcutta:

> Our sisters had to go to the home for the dying. And before they went, I said to them, "See, you are

---

[7] Teresa of Calcutta, *No Greater Love*, ed. Becky Benante and Joseph Durepos (Novato, CA: New World Library, 2002), 115.

going there, during Mass"—we always have Mass and Holy Communion in the morning before we go—and I said, "You saw during Holy Mass with what tenderness, with what love, father was touching the Body of Christ. Make sure, it is the same body in the poor that you will be touching."[8]

We cannot do true good without God's acting in and through us, and conversely, we cannot expect to become like God without manifesting that union in how we live and treat our neighbor. To live the Christian life is not simply to go about doing good without true consecration; nor is the Christian life exhausted by a silent and private union without a thirst for the almsdeeds. Our works of justice must be informed by divinization, and our heavenly rebirth must be made real by how we choose to live this life on earth.

In so doing, the Church teaches, we are only delivering God's goods to us to those who also deserve a share in our blessings. All those made in his divine image and likeness have a right to basic human goods, the goods of the body, the goods of friendship, the goods of a life recognized as fully human. This means that we who are blessed in abundance must pray to have deified eyes to see and thus serve Christ in those who are currently being cheated out

[8] Teresa of Calcutta, *Where There Is Love, There Is God* (New York: Doubleday Religion, 2010), 167.

of their God-given desire not to find this life a burden:

> St. John Chrysostom vigorously recalls this: "Not to enable the poor to share in our goods is to steal from them and deprive them of life. The goods we possess are not ours, but theirs [*De Lazaro Concio*, II, 6: PG 48, 992D]". "The demands of justice must be satisfied first of all; that which is already due in justice is not to be offered as a gift of charity [*Apostolicam Actuositatem* §5.8]": "When we attend to the needs of those in want, we give them what is theirs, not ours. More than performing works of mercy, we are paying a debt of justice [St. Gregory the Great, *Regula Pastoralis*, III. 21]." (CCC §2446)

What makes social justice into the almsdeeds of the Holy Spirit, the corporal and spiritual works of mercy, is not more efficiency but charity. It is good and right that all humans watch out for their neighbors' basic needs, but Christians are called to do these actions with a purity of intention and with an eye toward the eternal well-being of all whom the Lord puts into their lives.

CHAPTER 9

MARY, FULL OF GRACE (LUKE 1:38)

Because of Mary's "yes," the Son of God is no longer just "everywhere." He is now "somewhere." Mary's fidelity localizes the Son's presence: he is now here and not there, in this body and not that one. This is what the early Church had to come to terms with, what Christian naysayers called "the scandal of the particular." *You mean to tell me that this carpenter of Nazareth is the Messiah? This uneducated, little city boy is really the Savior of the world? How can the fullness of divinity be isolated, located, in this one man?* It was a Love too familiar, too close, too particular. But the truth is, the Son of God entrusted himself to a human family. "Family" and "familiarity" share the same root, and we all know what "familiarity" breeds: contempt. It is much safer to have a God who just stays off in the heavens, who is recognizable only by the extraordinary and the pyrotechnic.

As we begin to close this slender volume, we end with

where our Heavenly Father began, the Blessed Virgin Mary. It is here the Father falls in love with each of us, protecting her from the stain of sin in order that, through her "yes," he could take up dwelling and thus reunite all of humanity into the sacred humanity of his Son. In the person of Mary, the Church beholds a vibrantly manifold union with God: here is the Father's perfect daughter, the Son's loving mother, and the faithful bride of the Holy Spirit. She is at once what all saints will eventually become—a beloved child of God, a mighty bearer of Christ, and a docile dwelling of the Spirit. This chapter will, therefore, offer some helpful images of Mary as we continue to contemplate the Christian life as one of union and allowing God's own life to be formed in us now and forever.

Daughter of the Father

In his poem "The Virgin," the English poet William Wordsworth (d. 1850) called Mary "our tainted nature's solitary boast," as she alone has escaped the degradation of original sin and emerges as the one human person who has been plucked by God's grace from the effects of the Fall. Against all theologies of merit and unhealthy spiritualities of somehow deserving or earning God's grace, the life of the Blessed Virgin Mary is one of grace through and through. Descended from Adam and Eve, Mary, too, was destined to the lot of original sin, but through the free gift of God's providential love, she was instead saved from the effects of the Fall for the sake of God's very Son. In so becoming, one of the earliest images for Mary in the Christian Tradition is "the New Eve."

It was the bishop and martyr St. Irenaeus who, in the second century, saw in Mary another woman, sinless like Eve before the Fall, who has been conceived in order to help re-gather the human race into Christ. St. Irenaeus understood how the Father did not give up on the dying and divided human race but, in our Lady, began anew to reverse the effects of sin and disobedience:

> For just as Eve was led astray by the word of an angel, so that she fled from God when she had transgressed his word; so did Mary, by an angelic communication, receive the glad tidings that she would bear God, being obedient to his word. And if Eve did disobey God, yet Mary was persuaded to be obedient to God, in order that the Virgin Mary might become the patroness (*advocata*) of the virgin Eve. And thus, as the human race fell into bondage to death by means of a virgin, so it is rescued by a virgin.[1]

The saintly story of Mary begins in the womb of her moth-

---

[1] Irenaeus, *Against Heresies* 5.19; trans. Alexander Roberts and James Donaldson, in *Ante-Nicene Fathers*, vol. 1 (Peabody, MA: Hendrickson Publishers [1885] 2004), 547.

er, whom sacred tradition has named Anna. It is a central part of this tradition that, from the moment of Mary's conception, God the Father preserved her from the taint of original sin, in her fashioning a new ark for a new covenant, an unsullied dwelling place for the life of his Son.

Here, beginning with the formation of this tiny little girl, is the greatest of all dramas, the story of the Christ and the redemption of the human race. But hers is actually a story that began back in the Garden of Eden, when the first human couple (also created immaculately) contained the entirety of the human race in themselves. Unlike other creatures, the story of Genesis depicts humanity coming from one ultimate head, Adam, from whose side Eve is brought (see Gen 2:21–22) and from them, all other men and women. Unlike the sub-human animals whom God created in pairs, Adam, as sole "head," signifies an even deeper unity among the human family than any other species of creature. When sin entered the human race, then the consequence of Adam and Eve's forfeiting the organic harmony intended for the human race was disastrous. The wholeness God desired for those made in his image and likeness came to an abrupt—but not irredeemable—end.

Henceforth, the human race was marked by division and discord. As an illustration, call to mind two natural "bookends" of the Christian story—namely, the birth and the death of the man Jesus Christ. At Christmas we hear that "a child is born to us" (Isa 9:5) and on Good Friday we see in the death of Christ our death to sin, the cancellation of all our sins. How different is this birth; how different is this death. For when another person is born in the world, we are happy and join in on the celebration, but we remain fairly unchanged; when another person in the world dies and we express our condolences to friends and family, we are saddened but not wholly altered. But in Christ's birth, we, too, are reborn; in Christ's death, we, too, have our sins put to death. This is because Christ is the "New Adam," the One in whom all children of Adam and Eve have been regathered, reunited as a family. After the Fall, God tried other means of reconciliation—the beauty of creation, the Law, the Prophets and judges of the Old Testament, great kings like David, and so on—but nothing was able to restore the concord he desired. Unwilling to give up on the human race, in "the fullness of time" (Gal 4:4), the Father sent his Son from heaven into the womb of Mary through the overshadowing of the Holy Spirit and, in so doing, reunited all of his children in the sacred humanity of his Son Jesus Christ.

But a question arose in the history of theology: From where did the Son of God receive all of humanity? How was the Son of God able to unite to himself the entire human condition? How could one man regather all disparate and dying humanity? The answer is, of course, from the one from whom he received his humanity, his mother Mary. But where did she receive all of humanity? The Catholic answer, which had been a popular thought across the centuries, received its final form in the Dogma of the Immaculate Conception. As one saved from the death and division of the Fall, Mary is conceived as the New Eve in whom all will be recapitulated under her maternal intercession. It was first in the womb of Mary, in the unqualified "yes" of Mary, that humanity had been regathered:

> Indeed it was wholly fitting that so wonderful a mother should be ever resplendent with the glory of most sublime holiness and so completely free from all taint of original sin that she would triumph utterly over the ancient serpent. To her did the Father will to give his only-begotten Son— the Son whom, equal to the Father and begotten by him, the Father loves from his heart—and to give this Son in such a way that he would be the one and the same common Son of God the Father and of the Blessed Virgin Mary. It was she whom the Son himself chose to make his Mother and it was from her that the Holy Spirit willed and brought it about that he should be conceived and born from whom he himself proceeds.[2]

---

[2] Pope Pius IX, Apostolic Constitution on the Immaculate Conception *Ineffabilis Deus* (December 8, 1854), §1.

Mary alone was provided with the special graces needed to keep her from sinking into the morass of sin and decrepitude of fallen humanity. This saving should again be stressed as a liberation brought about from the moment of Mary's conception *not* out of her own virtue or merit, but because she was the future mother whom the Father desired would carry his Son into the world.

Everything the Church teaches about Our Lady ultimately has to do with the Person of Christ. She points us to him as he in turn points us back to her. In the East, she is invoked as *Panagia*, the "All Holy," because of Gabriel's referring to her as one "full of grace," (Luke 1:28), meaning there is room for nothing else in her but God's favor (see CCC §493). God saved Mary in a very unique way ("my spirit rejoices in God *my Savior.*" Luke 1:47) because in his utter humility, he chose to need her to become the human mother of his Only-Begotten Son. "[N]o evil shall befall you, no affliction come near your tent" (Ps 91:10). While the Lord has interacted with sinners since the time of our expulsion from Eden, in Mary's humanity, he needed a proverbial beachhead by which he was able to come to us personally and physically and thus gather through her all the wild and ropey sinners who had strayed far from the Father's family.

Whereas the first two major Church councils (Nicaea in 325 and the First Council of Constantinople in 381) had to answer questions concerning the Persons of the Holy Trinity, the next ecumenical gathering—the Council of Ephesus in 431—turned to the motherhood of Mary. Some heretical Christian leaders forbade their congregations from invoking Mary as the "Mother of God," but the Church rose up to defend this ancient title. Human mothers transmit their humanity to their children, and since the One whom Mary bore in her womb and gave birth to in Bethlehem is, in fact, God-made-man, she is truly the Mother of God, the Son now incarnate. She is, of course, neither the Mother of the Father nor the Mother of the Holy Spirit, but Mother of the incarnate Christ, who has come to redeem the world in its entirety. One last consideration arose from these early musings on Mary: a mother also provides the first examples of love and acceptance. In keeping the mother of his own Son free from all sin and bias, from every possible bad example and from every uncharitable word or feeling, the Father saw it most fitting that Jesus would grow up in a home unsullied by prejudice or any unrighteousness.

Spouse of the Holy Spirit

The Father preserved Mary from sin not for her own salvation but in order that he could send his Spirit to her and thus conceive in Mary's womb the Savior. This mystical union between Mary and the Holy Spirit is the prototype and the pattern of what our Father wants to do with every human person: to win over our love, to manifest his life in us, to incarnate his Son in our very lives, and to have us reign in his heaven forever.

Have you ever noticed how the priest at Mass places his hands over the bread and wine on the altar and prays in one form or another: "Be pleased, O God, we pray, to bless, acknowledge, and approve this offering in every respect; make it spiritual and acceptable, so that it may become for us the Body and Blood of your most beloved Son, our Lord Jesus Christ" (Eucharistic Prayer I), or, perhaps more familiarly, "You are indeed Holy, O Lord, the fount of all holiness. Make holy, therefore these gifts, we pray, by sending down your Spirit upon them like the dewfall, so that they may become for us the Body and Blood of our Lord Jesus Christ" (Eucharistic Prayer II)? This *epiclesis* (Greek for "calling down") is the sacramental continuation of the Holy Spirit's overshadowing of Mary's ovum, effecting the same outcome: taking what was once natural and impersonal, Mary's womb, and transforming it into One who is now supernatural and personal, the Messiah, God now finally with us in the flesh. The Spirit of God continues to incarnate the Son in the innermost chamber of our Mother, the Church.

What significance does this moment have for Christians? How is Mary's being found worthy of such divine inhabitation affect our discipleship and love of the Lord? Mary reminds us how the divine Persons of the Trinity love to include us creatures in their work of salvation. God will delegate to his creatures endowed with free will whatever he can. I remember one day during seminary studies back in Austria, I was walking down a picturesque Alpine street, and, obviously seeing my Roman collar, a local excitedly ran up to me and asked, "Is God everything for you?" Perhaps he was looking for a Christian hero, someone for whom this world must not matter much. I could see my answer disappointed him, "No. God is not everything. If he were, you and I and all this majestic beauty would be nothing." And then I cited 1 Corinthians 15:28, that God longs to "be all in all." In other words, in one way, God is the fullness of all reality, but when God chose to create, he chose not to be everything but hoped we would find his fullness in everything else he has given us.

Mary's own life is what ours, too, will become, hers through conception, ours through purgation. She is sinless, and we are not, but we are all called to bear the Christ in our lives in whatever way the Holy Spirit bids us. The Spirit of God was drawn to the outstanding virtues and the prayer pose of this young woman of Nazareth, and through her beauty, the Father now sees all of us as his daughters and sons. Mary is the lens through whom the Father sends his Son into the world in order to make us the same in our unique, creaturely way. The Jesuit poet Gerard Manley Hopkins, S.J. (d. 1889) put this ongoing

life into a most wonderful poem, "The Blessed Virgin
Compared to the Air We Breathe":

> Of her flesh He took flesh:
> He does take fresh and fresh,
> Though much the mystery how,
> Not flesh but spirit now
> And makes, O marvelous!
> New Nazareths in us,
> Where she shall yet conceive
> Him, morning, noon, and eve;
> New Bethlems, and He born
> There, evening, noon, and morn—
> Bethlem or Nazareth,
> Men here may draw like breath
> More Christ and baffle death;
> Who, born so, comes to be
> New self and nobler me
> In each one and each one
> More makes, when all is done,
> Both God's and Mary's Son.

In espousing himself to Our Lady, the Holy Spirit's love
flows through her—through his Church—into each of us.
Our response must therefore be a daily and firm "yes" to
God, and in so doing we continue Mary's "may it be done
to me" in our own soul.

One of the great saints to lead us further into the implications of the Spirit's coming to Mary and to us in this way is St. Louis de Montfort (d. 1716). Living in a time of great skepticism and antipathy against Christianity, St. Louis de Montfort labored to turn the minds of his fellow Frenchmen falling away from the Faith back through Mary to Christ. "It was through the Blessed Virgin Mary that Jesus Christ came into the world. And it is also through her that he must reign in the world."[3] Mary is the "neck" connecting Christ our Head with us his Body. This is a union inaugurated by the Annunciation and continued through the Church's sacraments and our own prayerful surrender. It is a union uniquely incarnational in Bethlehem but not limited to there, as the Holy Spirit will draw personally and mystically to anyone who is open to an increase of his divine presence.

Mother of the Son

It is in Mary we first come to behold the face of God literally. This incarnate God longs to present each of us to his Mother as her own sons and daughters. We see this first when he is told that she and his siblings are looking for him. "But he said in reply to the one who told him, 'Who is my mother? Who are my brothers?' And stretching out his hand toward his disciples, he said, 'Here are

---

[3] Louis de Montfort, *True Devotion to Mary*, §1.

my mother and my brothers. For whoever does the will of my heavenly Father is my brother, and sister, and mother'" (Matt 12:48–50).

The Cistercian Fr. Simeon (Erasmo Leiva-Merikakis) points out that it is highly significant to notice that Jesus refrains from calling any human person "Father" but instead orients us toward the intimacy of motherhood:

> The passage (Matt 12:48–50) is clearly establishing that, while Jesus has one Father only, the one who is in heaven, he wishes to make all believers partakers in what his Mother already is: one so receptive to the Word of God that she conceived this Word at the center of her being and brought it forth as the gift for the world's salvation. In other words, while the Father's divine paternity is wholly transcendental and incomparable, Mary's human maternity, though real and essential to redemption, is nonetheless the quality of a creature, and, as a creaturely quality, it is possible for others to participate in it.

Thus, the humanity of Jesus, fashioned by the Spirit out of the Virgin's obedience and faith and body, is the "place" where God and man meet, in such a way that the life of the eternal Trinity becomes embodied in our human flesh. In a real sense, like Mary, we may conceive Jesus through faith and bear him back to the Father by giving him birth in this world. The Church is the family in which what has already happened to Mary is extended, by participation, to all of God's children, who thus became Mary's children as well.[4]

The Church is the family of God, and what is a family without a mother? What a family who has a perfect mother! At the Second Vatican Council, the Church insisted that we accept Mary as "our mother in the order of grace,"[5] and if we are members of her Son's Body—contemporary prolongations of her Son's own life—Mary must be approached, invoked, and received as our mother too.

In his work on consecrated virginity, St. Augustine reflected beautifully on how our incorporation into the Body of Christ rendered Mary our supernatural mother: "She is the mother of Christ's members, which is ourselves, since she has cooperated with charity for the birth of the faithful in the Church. They are the members of that head, but she is physically the mother of the head himself. So it was fitting that by a unique miracle our

---

[4] Ersamo Leiva-Merikakis, *Fire of Mercy: Heart of the World. Volume II (chs. 12–18): Meditations on the Gospel According to Matthew* (San Francisco: Ignatius Press, 2003), 174–75.

[5] This term appears twice in *Lumen Gentium* §61 and §62.

head was born physically from a virgin, to signify that his members would be born spiritually from the virgin Church."[6] In her universal maternity, Mary not only models but helps to mold us into the glorified Church for which her Son died.

As such, let us never think of Mary as somehow immaculately above the pain and the tears of living in this fallen world. The devotion to her Seven Sorrows bespeaks the faithful's understanding that their mother wept more than most, felt more than most, cried out for justice more than anyone. For it is Mary's yes that allowed God himself to take on all of our sufferings, and nowhere does Christianity shy away from the brutal reality of what it meant for these two perfect people to live in a world of malice, selfishness, and murder. In fact, one wonders if at that moment of angelic invitation, Mother Mary had a sense and maybe an internal dialogue with the Lord: *If you are Infinite, the only thing I can give you is smallness; if you, Yahweh, are Immortal, the only thing I can give you is mortality; if you are Life, the only thing I can give you is death.* As the unmatchable mystical theologian Caryll Houselander (d. 1954) reflected, "Christ is life; dead did not belong to him. In fact, unless Mary would give him death, he could not die. Unless she would give him the capacity for suffering, he could not suffer. He could feel

---

[6] Augustine of Hippo, *On Virginity*, §6.

cold and hunger and thirst if she gave him her vulnerability to cold and hunger and thirst."[7] And so it was, and
so it is. The Lord Jesus Christ and his Mother do not run
away from smallness and littleness, from humility, insults,
scorn, and death. In fact, they embrace it only to redeem
it. Every child enters the world in order to draw breath,
but One came into the world to breathe his last.

In so doing, the incarnate Son of God has chosen to
live like us in all things "yet without sin" (Heb 4:15). Because of Mary's grace in reuniting all humanity offered
to her Son in her most blessed womb, the Son of God is
enabled to thus become the New Adam because, "just as
through the disobedience of one person the many were
made sinners, so through the obedience of one the many
will be made righteous. The law entered in so that trans-
gression might increase but, where sin increased, grace
overflowed all the more, so that, as sin reigned in death,
grace also might reign through justification for eternal life
through Jesus Christ our Lord" (Rom 5:19–21). Although
the eternal life for which we were made slipped through
the sinful hands of Adam and Eve, squandered and lost
for the rest of us who were meant to enjoy it, through the
hands of the New Adam and the New Eve, we are able to
receive an even greater intimacy with God.

---

[7] Caryll Houselander, *The Reed of God* (South Bend, IN: Ave Maria
Press [1944] 2006), 72–73.

Both biblical theology as well as popular piety over the centuries see Mary as the "woman . . . with the moon under her feet, and on her head a crown of twelve stars" (Rev 12:1). As we all know, the moon has no luminosity of its own but reflects the sun's light. Mary's supernatural existence is nothing other than the reflection of her Son Jesus who is the fountain and the source of all Mary is and does. The final words of Mary recorded in Sacred Scripture, "Do whatever he tells you" (John 2:5), point us to the Christ-life she commands us to have as well. As she mirrors her Son perfectly, we, too, are called to be transformed as much into Christ as our own fallible selves will freely allow. But here is the great paradox; she not only presents her Son to the world; in turn, he presents his mother back to us: "Behold, your mother" (John 19:27). In sharing his own mother with us, God once again proves his love and does what he can to win over ours. In making Mary our mother too, God has given us access to the most powerful human person ever to have lived. Regardless of our beginnings, regardless of how precarious our own upbringing may have been, each of us now has a mother in whom we can find acceptance, warmth, and hope that we too can love and be loved perfectly.

CHAPTER 10

Moving Now from Grace to Grace (2 Cor 3:18)

This short book has tried to lay out the entire reason and goal of the Christian life: for us to receive Christ in such a way that we begin to continue his life in the world as he continues his Incarnation in us. Together he and we form one mystical person, one huge family, the Church. Made in his image and likeness, we are already destined for a life in God; however, created with the freedom to reject our deepest longings, we do not necessarily have to choose to live this Christ-life. Most days we do choose, then we turn away, and then we come back, and so on. We are fickle, half-hearted creatures who can be too easily swayed to grow comfortable with what really should be uncomfortable. But St. Paul asks us to move "from glory to glory" (2 Cor 3:18), so as these pages come to a close, let us ask how this might be done.

The Lord will accept us as we are whenever we let

him. He will receive our erratic and unconvinced hearts if we only let him. He is not afraid of our various sicknesses, nor does he fear descending into our broken lives. In fact, an ancient homily from Holy Saturday centuries and centuries ago depicts this descent into our man-made hells with chilling illustrations and profound insight, as we will see in the following section.

The Church Waiting: Holy Saturday's Stillness

I have always thought the Church lives in a constant Holy Saturday: we have all known death and disease, we have all known various "crucifixions" in our lives, but we have not yet really reached the fullness of Easter glory. We are a Church on pilgrimage who must journey patiently in the virtue of hope. Recall that nervous waiting of any Holy Saturday and bring to mind the Church's teaching that between the Cross and the Tomb, Christ descended into hell (see 1 Pet 4:6) to let his power be known to those who died before his Incarnation. Whoever was willing to be led out, humbly acknowledging that life was not meant to be lived in the darkness of despair and the Sheol of sin, could arise with the Crucified Savior:

> Something strange is happening—there is a great silence on earth today, a great silence and stillness. The whole earth keeps silence because the King is asleep. The earth trembled and is still because God

has fallen asleep in the flesh and he has raised up all who have slept ever since the world began. God has died in the flesh and hell trembles with fear.

He has gone to search for our first parent, as for a lost sheep. Greatly desiring to visit those who live in darkness and in the shadow of death, he has gone to free from sorrow the captives Adam and Eve, he who is both God and the son of Eve. The Lord approached them bearing the cross, the weapon that had won him the victory. At the sight of him Adam, the first man he had created, struck his breast in terror and cried out to everyone: "My Lord be with you all." Christ answered him: "And with your spirit." He took him by the hand and raised him up, saying: "Awake, O sleeper, and rise from the dead, and Christ will give you light."

"I am your God, who for your sake have become your son. Out of love for you and for your descendants I now by my own authority command all who are held in bondage to come forth, all who are in darkness to be enlightened, all who are sleeping to arise. I order you, O sleeper, to awake. I did not create you to be held a prisoner in hell. Rise from the dead, for I am the life of the dead. Rise up, work of my hands, you who were created in my image. Rise, let us leave this place, for you are in me and I am in you; together we form only one person and we cannot be separated."[1]

We have seen this paradox over and over again: God is drawn not to the perfect and righteous but to the sinner, to those dead who hide for fear of what the light might reveal.

But as we grow more and more in love with Christ, we are weaned ever more from our own sniveling, sinful selves. Only in this encounter can we finally be transformed into the fullness of the image in whom we were made in the first place. We must have no other response to the divine initiative, as this is how we are to understand the full meaning of the Incarnation: God loves us so much that he longed to become like us, and we, in turn, must become like him. St. Paul knew this all too well, realizing that, "All of us, gazing with unveiled face on the glory of the Lord, are being transformed into the same image from glory to glory, as from the Lord who is the Spirit" (2 Cor 3:18). Whether we call this transformation "deification," "divinization," "theosis," "sanctification," or even "growing in holiness," this is a Christification which empowers mere mortals to do immortal things, for humans to live superhumanly, to live as Christ and as he would have us do.

---

[1] Ancient Holy Saturday Homily as found in the Office of Readings for Holy Saturday, *The Liturgy of the Hours*, vol. II (New York: Catholic Book Publishing Co., 1975), 496–97.

Victory through Emptying

The initiative and the grace to live as Christ is all his. In the kenotic hymn of Philippians 2, the Church sings of the Son's emptying (*kenosis*) of his divinity in order to take on our humanity. Imagine what this experience would be like: to leave the glory and perfection of heaven to be born in a stable under the tyranny of injustice and persecution. Imagine what it would be like to be God but now to have to learn to speak, walk, and read, and all that goes into becoming fully human. But this letting go of his divinity did not stop in the lone figure of Jesus Christ. This emptying continues in each of us weak and frail disciples. Christ continues to stumble and fall in each of our well-intentioned but less than perfect attempts to proclaim the Father's love to the world. But this is a hidden aspect of the Good News: Christ would rather have our cooperation and involvement in helping save souls than he would have the perfection with which he could save the cosmos in the blink of an eye. The Son of God has thus chosen to see his truest and fullest self only with us in communion with him.

This is why Vatican II's call for the entire Church to evangelize and become holy was such a needed recognition. This "universal call to holiness" must be lived out by all who read these pages, not just clerics or religious. You have a credibility and an authority that the professionally religious do not. People expect us to talk about God. People do not think we priests or nuns know what the "real world" is like. But when you, who have raised your families, paid your mortgages, and lived lives immersed in the world, speak about Christ and the freeing invitation of his Church to become like him, people listen. This is why the Father has given you the family you have, the career you have, the neighborhood and community you have. This is why you were born when you were: your life is like no other, and through your unification with his Son, the Father pleads that you live Christ's life by loving those he puts into this very life of yours.

Most of us will feel very deficient and unworthy. So we are. But as long as my attention is on my own capabilities, I shall always feel inadequate to be an evangelist. But if I can turn my attention to who the Lord is and what he wants to accomplish in and through me, I simply have to let him:

He belongs to you, but more than that, he longs to be in you, living and ruling in you, as the head lives and rules in the body. He desires that whatever is in him may live and rule in you: his breath in your breath, his heart in your heart, all the faculties of his soul in the faculties of your soul, so that these words may be fulfilled in you: *Glorify God and bear him in your body, that the life of Jesus may be made manifest in you.*[2]

This desire for unity is twofold: Christ longs to be one with us just as much—if not exponentially more—as we desire our perfection in him. It is this divine desire we often ignore. Is it too awesome for our mortal minds to behold? The Lord Jesus Christ has chosen to extend his sacrificial offering of self to each of us. In Christ our head, we too offer ourselves to the Father at every Mass, in every act of charity and in every moment of prayer.

This means we need to ask the Holy Spirit to show us how we can make time for personal prayer each day. What can we change in our busy schedules so as to make room for more time with Jesus? Are we able to get to early morning Mass throughout the week, thereby giving our day a certain ritual and pattern and our souls a certain accountability and certainly increased peace? Maybe we can give God only a portion of our daily commute. If so, turn off the radio and put away the phone and talk to the Holy Spirit (even out loud, if that helps) as a friend traveling to or from work each day.

This also means we need to grow in self-awareness in order to detect where we are growing in union as Christ's

---

[2] John Eudes, *Heart of Jesus*, Book 1.5, as found in the Office of Readings for August 19, his Feast Day, in the *Liturgy of the Hours*, vol. IV (New York: Catholic Book Publishing Co., 1975), 1331.

Body and where we are still preferring words and images and actions less than what Christ can offer. Where do we sin, and what do we do about it? A monthly confession is not out of the question, thus providing a regular check-up in dialogue with one who might counsel and who can certainly forgive us. Too, how are we spending our time? Do we tend to wander, content to flit about things that are superficial and increasingly ephemeral—internet sites, television programs, social media platforms which leave us restless and more politically divisive? Pay attention to how you are nourishing your eternal soul.

Christ is not complete without any one of us. That is why he gave his very lifeblood, so that we would melt before such a love and accept him so wholeheartedly that our lives would become one. This is the nature of the Church, and in the many grains of the Eucharist and in the countless grapes contained in the chalice, we see a mirroring of who we are all to become as well. That is why we who receive the Body of Christ must become evermore the Body of Christ by loving one another:

> The Eucharist commits us to the poor. To receive in truth the Body and Blood of Christ given up for us, we must recognize Christ in the poorest, his brethren: "You have tasted the Blood of the Lord, yet you do not recognize your brother. . . . You dishonor this table when you do not judge

worthy of sharing your food someone judged worthy to take part in this meal. . . . God freed you from all your sins and invited you here, but you have not become more merciful. (CCC §1397, quoting St. John Chrysostom, *Homily on 1 Corinthians*, §27.4)

Since God became human, we can return to God only through the human. This is why love of God and love of neighbor are absolutely inseparable. The care and reverence we show Jesus in his Blessed Sacrament must be extended to all those living flesh and blood neighbors he himself has put into our lives.

Christ chooses to do nothing apart from his Church, and his Church can obviously achieve nothing good apart from Christ. We must not take our baptism, our prayer life, our daily routine and expenditures of time and treasure, our reception of the Most Sacred Host, or all those lost opportunities for the grace of Reconciliation too lightly. We are called to receive Christ so as to become him, and this alone will determine our eternal destinies.